SZECHUAN COOKING

WEATHERVANE BOOKS
New York

Published 1985 by Weathervane Books, distributed by
Crown Publishers, Inc.

Printed in Taipei, Taiwan, R.O.C.

ISBN 0-517-47512X
h g f e d c b a

SZECHUAN COOKING
CONTENTS

Notes:
1. Each dish makes 6 servings.
2. In most cases, the quantity of seasonings used can be adjusted to your taste.
3. To prepare stock, boil 10 ounces lean pork, 10 ounces pork ribs, 5 ounces ham, 1 ounce small dried shrimps, 1 slice ginger, 1 star anise, 1 slice dried orange peel, and $3\frac{1}{2}$ large soup bowls of water over a low flame to make a large soup bowl of stock. Strain through cheesecloth.
4. Continue to cook a dish briefly after adding cornstarch paste, to thicken the sauce.

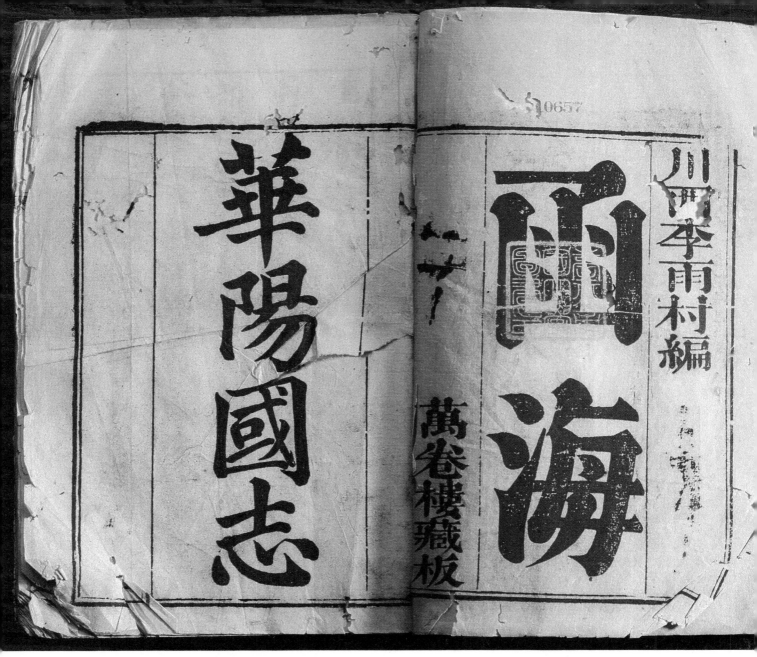

THE HISTORY AND CUSTOMS OF SZECHUAN

Szechuan's old name is Ba-Shu, because it consisted of the Ba State and the Shu State. Though it is located at the southwest of China, it started to communicate with the Central Plain Area in very early days. According to the history, Huangti's son, Changi, married a woman from the Shu State.

Ba-Shu was a very civilized place even in ancient times. The people in Ba-Shu knew the techniques of making copperware and farming and the ways of weaving silk in the 15th century.

During the period of Warring States, all states had counties set up at the border for self-defense. When Ba and Shu were exterminated by the Chin State, Chin immediately changed their names to Ba County and Shu County and had 10,000 of Chin's citizens moved to these two counties. And Cheng-Du was reconstructed according to

the city plan of Hsien-Yang, the capital of Chin, at that time by the order of the Prime Minister of Chin State, Chang Yi. The prosperity and wealth of Ba-Shu helped Chin unify China.

In the reign of Emperor Ching of the West Han Dynasty, the magistrate of Shu County sent several local literates to Chang-An to study. After they graduated from Chang-An, these scholars were assigned to be educators of the locals of Szechuan. Szechuan thus became an educated land, with many famous scholars.

Yi-Chou, the name of Cheng-Du during the Han and Tang dynasties, was the richest city in the Tang Dynasty. Emperor Hsuan of the Tang Dynasty fled to Szechuan when An Lu-shan and Shih Sze-ming rebelled. He renamed Cheng-Du "Nan-Chin," meaning the southern capital. Cheng-Du stayed the only peaceful place during the rebellion, because of its wealth.

The two most famous poets in the history of China are Lee Bai, the Immortal Poet, who was born and raised in Szechuan, and Du Fu, the Sage Poet, who spent most of his life in Szechuan. It is believed that the elegant and majestic landscape and the rich and abundant prairie of Szechuan had a strong influence on their great poetry.

In the time of the Five Dynasties, Shu was the only rich and happy place when all other places were at war. Especially when Emperor Meng Chang was reigning, Cheng-Du was so rich that all kinds of flowers were planted all over the city, and Cheng-Du was once known as the City of Hibiscus.

There were many outstanding scholars in the Sung Dynasty, because Emperor Tai-Tsu paid great attention to the enhancement of literature. Of the Eight Great Scholars of the Tang and Sung dynasties, three were from Szechuan: Su Hsun, Su Shih (Su Tung-Po), and Su Che, the father-and-sons team. And Su Tung-Po was also a well-known gourmet. Several of his poems are on the culinary arts.

At the end of the Ming Dynasty, bandit leaders Chang Hsien-chung and Lee Tsu-cheng led an army to attack Szechuan several times. For the first time in its history, Szechuan became poor. When Chang Hsien-chung entered Cheng-Du, he set up a monument, saying that "Heaven sends us so many good things to raise us, but we have not done anything good to return heaven's favor. Therefore, I want to kill, kill, kill, kill, kill, kill, and kill." Szechuan did not regain its prosperity until the middle of the Ching Dynasty.

In the year 1937, the Sino-Japanese War began. R.O.C.'s government moved its base to Chungking. Relying on the abundant resources and human power of Szechuan, the government finally won this eight-year war.

1. The Traffic of Szechuan

Szechuan was named because it has four rivers, Ming River, Tou River, Chia-Ling River, and the Yangtze River, running through it. (The meaning·of Szechuan is four rivers.) Surrounded by very tall mountains, with a basin in the center, Szechuan is hard to approach either by land or by water.

The land of the basin of Szechuan is so rich that the local people can live independently and need not import anything to survive. Many instances can be found in the history of China to prove the saying that "Owning Szechuan is enough to fight against the world."

Since it is surrounded by high mountains, Szechuanese are confronted with the difficulty of traveling to other places. In one of his poem, "It's hard to leave Szechuan," Lee Bai wrote that to leave Szechuan is as hard as to go to heaven.

But Szechuan is no longer hard to approach or leave, and the saying "It's hard to leave Szechuan" is now historical, because of the road construction work provided by the R.O.C.'s government after the Chinese Civil War. Chungking is the center if you travel by water, and Cheng-Du is the center of land if you travel by land. Both highways and railroads take travelers into and out of Szechuan.

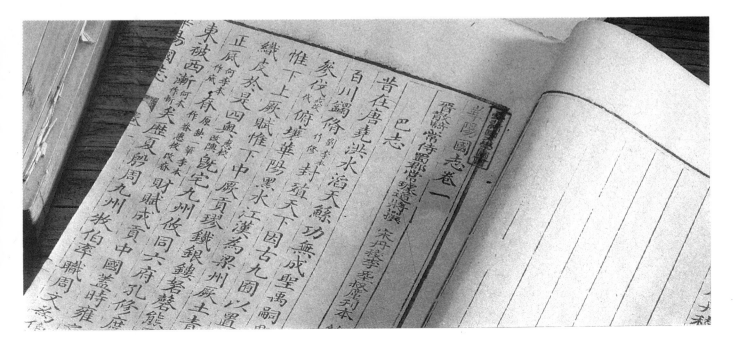

2. The Heavenly State

The many rivers running through Szechuan and the warm weather are the major reasons for Szechuan's prosperous farming business.

Its agricultural products are rice, sweet potatoes, sorghum, and soybeans in the summer, and rape, peas, kidney beans, barley, and wheat in the winter. Temperate fruits such as pears, peaches, and apples are the major products of northern Szechuan. Subtropical fruits such as oranges, longans, and lichees are the products of southern Szechuan. Szechuan's livestock industry is also booming. Pigs, lambs, cows, chickens, ducks, and geese are all raised.

On the mountain foot west to the basin, tea trees are planted. Meng-Ding tea is the best of all Szechuanese tea. Under the influence of the high temperature, sugarcane fields are wide and vast though Szechuan's latitude is high. Szechuan is also the number one district in China for the production of tung oil, medicinal herbs, hog bristles, white wax, and white fungus.

The major mineral resource of Szechuan is well salt. All the other provinces in the southwest of China import salt from Szechuan. With so many agricultural products, it is no wonder there is an old saying, "Szechuan will never have famine."

3. The Beautiful Three Mountains and Three Gorges

Szechuan's Scenery and Historical Spots

Having many mountains and many rivers, Szechuan's scenery is certainly gorgeous. Among its beautiful scenery, the Three Mountains, which are the graceful O-Mei Mountain, the elegant Ching-Cheng Mountain, and the precipitous Chien-Ke Mountain, and the Three Gorges are most worth visiting.

O-Mei Mountain

In Lee Bai's "Ode to the O-Mei Mountain" he said, "Among all the heavenly mountains in Shu State, O-Mei is the most beautiful one." Located at the southwest of Szechuan, its elevation is more than 3,300 meters. The name O-Mei was first used in the early age of Han Dynasty. It is named for the shape of the two opposite peaks. (O means lofty and Mei means eyebrows in Chinese.)

"Graceful" is the best adjective to describe O-Mei's scenery. From the mountain foot to its peak, the winding path is in the middle of woods, falls, and lakes. O-Mei has three peaks. The highest one is the Ten-Thousand-Buddhas Peak, the second highest is called the Golden Peak, and the third one is called Thousand-Buddhas Peak. The most famous scenic spots of O-Mei are "The Morning Rain at Hung-Chung," "The Overlapped Verdant Rocks," "The Sun and the Clouds at Lo-Feng," "White Water and Autumn Wind," "The Snow at Da-Ping," "The Twilight at Golden Peak," "The Evening Bell of the Sacred Temple," "Moonlight in the Elephant Pond," "The Quiet Two Bridges," and "The House of

Nine Elders." Temples and shrines of different sizes can be found in O-Mei Mountain. This is why O-Mei Mountain is one of the most famous Buddhist sites in China.

Ching-Cheng Mountain

Ching-Cheng Mountain is claimed to have 36 peaks, all facing east. Hermits of the Wai-Ching and Suei-Tang Dynasties liked to choose this mountain for their dwelling place.

Whether the hermits went to Ching-Cheng to get away from war or fame, living in the beautiful mountain day after day, as poets or painters they produced magnificent works.

If O-Mei is said to be the place for Buddhism, Ching-Cheng Mountain can be said to be the place for Taoism. In the period of the Five States, Taoism was very popular in Shu State. Therefore, many Taoist temples can be found in Ching-Cheng Mountain. Taoists call it the Fifth Dung-Tien.

Chien-Ke Mountain

Chien-Ke is a mountain chain at the north of Szechuan. It is famous for steep slopes and precipitous cliffs. And Chien-Men is the most dangerous place among all cliffs. In Lee Teh-Yu's "Ode to Chien-Men" it says, "Among all the westward-bound mountains, midst the heavy clouds, Chien-Men is a natural gate dangerous to pass to Shu State."

The log road along the cliffs built in the Han Dynasty was the only way out from Szechuan. Though it is no longer important, the cypress and the scenery along the road still attract many visitors.

Three Gorges

Running through Baiti City, the Yangtze River suddenly turns narrow. Water runs down for 200 meters from Feng-Chieh to Yi-Chang in a distance of 200 kilometers.

Kuei Gorge, Wu Gorge, and Hsi-Ling Gorge are the three most renowned gorges. The depth of these gorges is from 700 to 1,000 meters. It is said that "Sun and moon cannot be seen unless it is noontime or midnight when you are standing between the gorges." The saying tells of the steepness and narrowness of the cliffs.

Besides the Three Mountains and the Three Gorges, the world-famous Du-Chiang Levee, the Kung-Bu Cottage, where Du Fu wrote his poems, the Chia-Ding Buddha on Ling-Yun Mountain, and the Wang-Chiang Tower are also legendary historical spots in Szechuan.

"Boating by the Ba Gorge" Collection of the National Palace Museum

CHINESE CULINARY ART

1. Eating in China

(1) The Beginning

It was by accident that Peking Men learned how to make fire with two pieces of stone about 500,000 years ago. What is important about this accident is that human beings thus knew the meaning of having cooked food.

Chinese started to use oil to cook in about 3,000 years ago. Even before the year 1,000 B.C., the Chinese began to use soy sauce, vinegar, and spices to cook. Many methods were created to produce better and better food.

Till the Warring States, the art of cooking had been developed to a generous stage. In the book Lui's Chun-Chiu, the control of high, medium, and low flame and the ways of blending sour, sweet, bitter, and salty flavors are both described as delicate techniques.

Many foreign foods were brought into China during the Han Dynasty because of its vast land and busy communications with foreign countries on its west border. Pepper, chestnuts, and tomatoes were all imported goods at that time.

People of the Tang and Sung Dynasties were mostly wealthy. Cooking techniques and the banquet atmosphere had become more and more elaborate. The Recipes of Wei Chu-Yuan of the Tang Dynasty, Records of Food-Offerings of Wu Shih, and Yu-Kung-Pi of the chef of the Court of the Sung Dynasty are the records of the culinary art of the Tang and Sung dynasties.

In the freezing northen land of China, beef, mutton, and dairy products are the best food to provide energy.

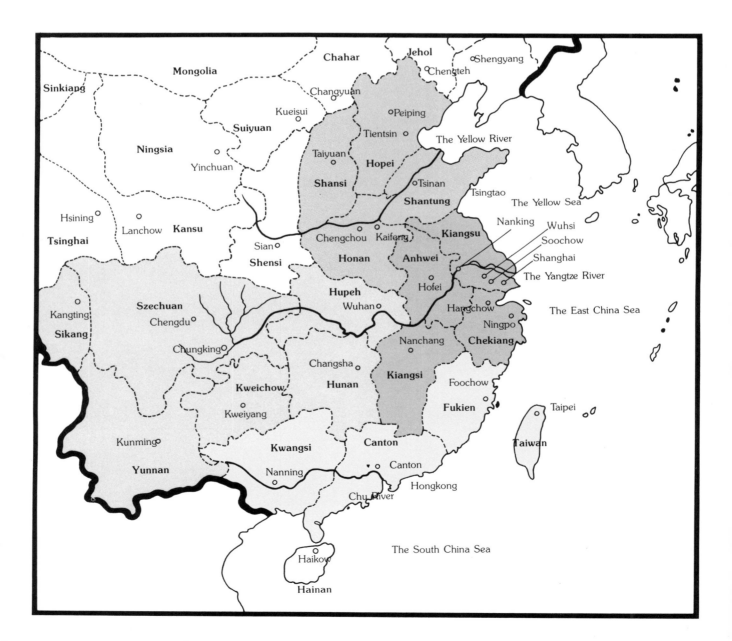

Together with the invasion of the Yuan's army, the habit of eating meat and dairy products was brought to China. Though it did not help in the improvement of cooking techniques, the book How to Eat Properly, edited by Hu Ssu-Hui, the Emperor's doctor of the Yuan Dynasty, is still one of the immortal books on Chinese culinary art.

The skills of cooking reached maturity in the Ching Dynasty. Yuan Mei's Suei-Yuan Recipes is the bible of culinary art. Delicious taste is no longer the only requirement of a good dish. The appearance of a dish is also considered essential. The extravagant Man-Han Banquet was created at that time. After 5,000 years of experience and improvements, Chinese culinary art finally became a special knowledge.

(2) Distribution

Regional foods with different taste were formed by the differences of weather, products, and customs.

Geographically speaking, the spreading of Chinese culinary art is along the banks of three major rivers: the Yellow River, the Yangtze River, and the Chu River. Divided by these three rivers, Chinese food can be separated into four regions. The first region is the area along the Yellow River. Peking dishes can best represent this region. The second region takes Szechuan as its center, with all those provinces along the western section of Yangtze River. The third region includes those provinces along the eastern section of the Yangtze River. Though Shanghai cuisine is to be claimed to be the center of this region, Yang-Chou dishes, Wu-Hsi dishes, Hang-Chou dishes, Ning-Po dishes, An-Huei dishes, and Kiang-Hsi dishes are also very special, with an original taste. The fourth region is along the bank of Chu River. This region includes Canton, Kuang-Hsi, Fukien, and Taiwan.

2. Taste of Szechuan

Cheng-Du dishes and Chungking dishes are representative of Szechuanese food. Having abundant farming and husbandry products, the Szechuanese like to cook their food with various methods and seasonings. Utilizing local products fully, even lichees, bananas, and dried orange peel are used to prepare a meal. Among all the seasonings used in Szechuanese dishes, the following six are the most popular and unique.

Red Oil

This is a mixture of chili oil, sesame oil, soy sauce, ground pepper, sesame sauce, minced spring onion, sugar, and minced garlic. Usually it is added to the half-cooked food during stir-frying.

Fish-Flavored Sauce (Fish-Fragrant)

The sauce is made by stir-frying sugar, vinegar, soy sauce, hot bean sauce, minced pepper, minced spring onion, minced garlic, and minced ginger. It can be poured on top of the cooked food or stir-fried with the major ingredient, then served.

Ma-La (Hot and Spicy)

Its major ingredients are ground pepper and chili. When it is used to make cold plate, soy sauce, vinegar, sesame oil, chili oil, ground pepper, minced spring onion, minced ginger, and sugar are mixed together, then poured over the major ingredients. For a hot stir-fried dish, add soy sauce, wine, vinegar, sugar, and chili powder during stir-frying. Sprinkle ground pepper on top before serving.

Sour and Hot

Just like its name, this seasoning features both sour and hot tastes. You can either boil the major ingredients with vinegar, sugar, chili, ground pepper, wine, salt, and soy sauce, or pour the mixture of soy sauce, vinegar, sesame oil, chili oil, minced spring onion, and minced ginger on top of the cooked major ingredients.

Dry-Fried

Stir-Fry major ingredients with chili powder, ground pepper, hot bean sauce, sugar, wine, salt, minced garlic, and minced spring onion over a low flame till cooked, then switch to a high flame and stir-fry till dry.

Strange-Flavored Sauce

This sauce is made by mixing sugar, minced spring onion, minced garlic, chili oil, soy sauce, ground pepper, sesame oil, and sesame sauce. It's called strange-flavored because the sauce tastes sweet, sour, hot, spicy, and salty at the same time.

IN MEMORY OF SZECHUANESE FOOD

(1) Restaurants and Food Stands

The geographic locations of Cheng-Du and Chungking are so good that these two places were very prosperous. Their prosperity can be imagined by their nicknames of "Small Peking" and "Small Shanghai." Besides many delicate banquet dishes served at several major restaurants, the delicious snacks served at some food stands were also unforgettable.

Rong-Le-Yuan Restaurant

This is located at Bu-Hou Street of Cheng-Du City. According to the late Mr. Chang Da-Chien, the famous painter and gourmet, Rong-Le-Yuan was owned by his former chef. Many Szechuanese dishes were created here, and many renowned chefs were trained here.

There was a saying that "Among all the famous chefs in Szechuan, Rong-Le-Yuan's chef is the best." At Rong-Le-Yuan, not only were banquet dishes served, but delicious homemade dishes were also available for family dining. Steamed Bear Palm, Soup of White Fungus and Quail Eggs, and Bean Sprout Buns were the most welcomed dishes.

Ku-Ku-Yen Restaurant

Huang Ching-Ling was an retire official of the Ching Dynasty. He lived in Cheng-Du after his retirement. Knowing that Mr. Huang was a generous person and that his chef's dishes were very good, some local rich men and officials liked to hold dinner parties at his home. Seeing that his chef's dishes were so well received, Mr. Huang decided to open up a restaurant. The name of the restaurant, "Ku-Ku-Yen," means that the dishes served there are not official.

The Drunken Royal Mistress, Liver Cake, and Stewed Squares were its best dishes.

Small Dung-Tien Restaurant

This is a famous old restaurant at Chungking. Originally built in a mountain cave, it was warm during winter and cold during summer. And it is named "Small Dung-Tien" because Dung-Tien means the space in a cave.

After moving several times, it finally settled down at Shin-Ban Street. Though its decorations were not as elegant as before, its food was still as good. First Class Crispy Squares, Chin-Chien Sea Cucumbers, Rice-Smoked Chicken, and Carp with Hot Bean Sauce were the most popular dishes.

Chen Ma-Po's Bean Curd Store

More than a hundred years ago, there was a small store owned by a widow, Mrs. Chen. Her homemade dishes were highly praised by her patrons. Near her store was the market for farm produce. The peddlers from the market liked to dine at her store. Usually the unsold stuff, such as oil, bean curd, and hot bean sauce, was given to Mrs. Chen to make dishes with.

Using these leftover ingredients, Mrs. Chen created a hot and spicy dish with bean curd as the major ingredient. Because there were some pockmarks on Mrs. Chen's face, these peddlers called this dish Ma-Po's Bean Curd. (Ma-Po means a woman with a pockmarked face in Chinese.) Earning her fame by this dish, Mrs. Chen decided to name her store "Chen Ma-Po's Bean Curd Store," selling bean curd and homemade dishes.

Lai Tang-Yuan's Food Stand

Lai is the family name of Lai Tang-Yuan's owner. Its tang-yuan was made by rolling stuffing in glutenous rice powder. Another famous item at Lai Tang-Yuan's was the Tang-Yuan-Fen made of glutenous rice and ordinary rice. The stuffing of Lai-Tang-Yuan's tang-yuan was made of iced orange, chicken oil, rose, and black sesame seeds. Delicious stuffing and nonsticky skin were the reasons Lai Tang-Yuan's tang-yuan was so welcomed.

Wu Chao-Shou

Chao-shou is also known as wonton. Wu is the family name of the owner of the wonton store. Wu's wontons featured thin skin and juicy stuffing.

Besides wontons, Wu Chao-Shou also sold some unique homemade dishes which were highly praised.

Dan-Dan-Mien

Dan-Dan-Mien is different from the Taiwanese Tan-Tzu Mien. The seasonings used in a small bowl of Dan-Dan-Mien include soy sauce, vinegar, lard, sesame oil, sesame sauce, bean sprouts, garlic juice, chili oil, ground pepper, minced spring onion, and ginger shreds. No wonder it is so delicious and tasty. The soup of Dan-Dan-Mien is also worth mentioning. It is pure chicken stock or stock of boiled pork ribs with bean sprouts. The soup itself is delicious without any seasoning.

(2) Teahouses and Wine Shops

Together with the delicious food, the tea and wine of Szechuan are the other two items that make the life of Szechuanese so delightful.

Teahouses

On the slopes by the basin of Szechuan, tea trees are spread around. The Meng-Ding tea from Meng-Ding Mountain is the best among all Szechuanese tea. The ancient Chinese believed that tea was good for eyes and mind.

Teahouses can be found in almost every corner of Szechuan. Going to teahouses in Szechuan is not only relaxing but also interesting. If a man of prestige comes to a teahouse, the waiter will greet him politely and say, "You are rich at home and during traveling, but coming to a teahouse can tell your wealth even better." If a poor man comes to the teahouse, the waiter will say, "Men shall walk up and let water run down," to encourage him.

The serving technique of the waiters in Szechuanese teahouses is also fascinating. Watching them pour water out of the large pot of boiling water into the small teapot is truly amusing.

Wine Shops

The most famous Szechuanese wine are Lu-Chou's Da-chiu wine and Mien-Chu's Da-chiu wine. Lu-Chou's Da-chiu wine, Shao-Hsing's Hua-diao wine, Shan-Hsi's Fen wine, Kuei-Chou's Mao-tai wine, and Tientsin's Wu-chia-pi are the five most famous wines of China.

Made from spring water, Lu-Chou's Da-chiu wine is sweet and clear. Szechuanese call wine making "wine baking." Wine shops are as common as teahouses in Szechuan. Szechuanese like to go to wine shops in the afternoon or at night. Chatting with friends in teahouses or wine shops is the Szechuanese way of relaxing. Of course, wine is not the only item sold in wine shops; small dishes like spiced bean curd, peanuts, and fried sticks are also served there.

Besides Da-chiu wine from Lu-Chou and Mien-Chu, the Wu-Shih-Kan wine of Chien-Wei County and the Lin wine and the Lang wine of Ku-Lin County are also very famous.

SZECHUANESE FOOD IN TAIPEI

1. The Story of Szechuanese Restaurants

The astonishing accomplishments of Taiwan in these thirty years has been regarded as an economic miracle by many people around the world. Besides its economic achievement, Taiwan is also well known for delicious Chinese food.

As Taipei is the economic, political, and cultural center of Taiwan, it is not surprising that Taipei gathers the best restaurants. Our story of Szechuanese restaurants will start with those oldest restaurants and their chefs. We would like to mention two famous chefs first. They are Wu Shao-Chen from Rong Shing Restaurant and Wai Cheng-Hsuan from Lien An Restaurant. Wu was an apprentice in a restaurant called Tao Yuan in Chungking first; then he went to Shanghai and joined the Chin Chiang Szechuanese Restaurant there. Wu came to Taiwan later and opened the first Szechuanese restaurant on this island, Tien Fu Restaurant, in 1946. Now Wu is the chef of Rong Shing Restaurant. As to Wei, his background is similar to Wu's. Wei was an apprentice in the Kai Kuo Gue Restaurant in Chungking. The restaurant was owned by Mr. Lee, a retired general who later played an important role in introducing Szechuanese food to Taiwan. After World War II, Mr. Lee invited Wai to lead the branch of Kao Kuo Gue Restaurant in Shanghai. In 1947, Wei came to Taiwan and acted as chef in Kai Kuo Gue Restaurant, Taipei. Kai Kuo Gue, located in Chung Shan S. Road, Taipei, gathered many good chefs who also had just moved from Mainland China to Taiwan. Wu and Wei are highly respected not only because they are

the teachers of many famous cooks nowadays but also because they dedicate their lives to Szechuanese cooking.

Lung Shiang Szechuanese Restaurant and Chin Chiang Szechuanese Restaurant were opened around 1950. Two other big restaurants at that time were Yue Yuang and O-Mei. The former was well decorated and thus became an important place for social meetings. The latter was famous among both the upper class and the ordinary people and set a milestone for the development of Szechuanese food in Taiwan. As time went by, more and more Szechuanese restaurants were established. Some of them are Chung Hwa, Hwa Shia, Ta Tung, Fu Hsiang, Tien I, Kuo Ting, Joan An, Chin Yuan, Ta Shun, King Ting, and Ambassador Hotel. The four restaurants we include in this book, Lien An Restaurant, Fortune Restaurant, Rong Shing Restaurant, and Jzyy Yuan Restaurant, are also the most well known ones. These restaurants are suitable not only for banquets but also for family gatherings. They are air-conditioned, well organized, and decorated with Chinese paintings and calligraphy. As these restaurants get bigger, they adopt modern kitchenware and scientific management in order to provide better service and to maintain their own growth. However, delicious food is still the important factor that determines the success of a restaurant. The most representative Szechuanese dishes include Stewed Beef Brisket over Wu-Ching Burner, Minced Garlic with White Pork, Stewed Pork Shreds with Fish-Flavored Sauce, Double-Cooked Pork, Dry-Fried French Beans, Kung-Bao

Chicken Dice, Ma-Po's Bean Curd, Ants Climbing Trees, Bean Curd, the Family Style, Steamed Pork Ribs Wrapped in Lotus Leaves, Stewed Shelled Shrimps with Kuo-Ba, and First Class Crispy Squares. And each restaurant has its own representative dishes.

Formal banquets must follow certain rules; for instance, the order of course dishes served cannot be reversed. Besides, the number of dishes and the interval between each course dish are already set. The quality of dishes, of course, depends on the set price customers choose.

The traditional spirit tablets worshiped by Chinese cooks. These spirits are Five-Roads Fortune God, Thunder God, God of Stove, and King Jan, the God of Royal Kitchen.

2. Luncheonettes and Beef Noodles

The enjoyment that a restaurant can give its customer includes nice service, delightful atmosphere, beautiful decoration, and most important of all, delicious dishes. It is the reason why some small restaurants and food stands attract hundreds of people and make a lot of profit. There are many famous luncheonettes for Szechuanese food in the downtown area, which provide nice places for a business lunch. Many of them are near Kanting Road, Omei Street, Min Sheng E. Road, Tunhua N. Road, Mandarin Hotel, Sec. 1 of Roosevelt Road and West Gate area. There are also some small Szechuanese luncheonettes near Taiwan University which are favored by young students. A special food stand worth mention here is Wu Chao-Shou, famous for its appetizers. Ning Gee Restaurant is well known for its firepot cooking. All these restaurants mentioned are popular because of strong-tasting dishes and low prices.

Beef noodles, Szechuanese style, is very popular in Taipei. It first was just a very ordinary kind of food offered by small food stands, but because of its hot taste and special flavor, it became a famous dish in Taipei, and even attracts many travelers from other countries.

Some of the food stands that first offered beef noodles are near National Normal University, at the intersection of Hsin-I Road and Hsin Sheng S. Road and Tao Yuan Street. Other famous ones include Liu Gee Beef Noodles in Tung Hua Street, Cheng's Beef Noodles in Yung Kang Street, a food stand near Kuo Hua Theater, Yung Ho, and Lao-Chang's near the intersection of Jen Ai Road and Hang-Chou S. Road.

青綠開山迴
崎嶇道路長
宋人名德意行
李自周祥說
高名利利那
翠芳與氏此
陳芳姓氏忙宗
近平唐
甲午新秋
尚題

"The Night Banquet" by Tseng Hou-Hsi   Collection of Ambassador Hotel

峨嵋劍閣
亞子の
天下出
雪道十人
谁興匹
者

五十六年葊
〇東四月和古
無軍香兵也
七句晋八山喬
浮手故鄉の山
以代尊淘之

歟

太白陝者
三已歷溢江
八汪園頓首

莘生

"The Four Mountains" by Chang Da-Chien
Transparencies Provided by the National Museum of History

19

聖母壽桃

The Celestial Peach Plate

Ingredients:
    3 prawns
    2¹/₂ ounces squid
    2¹/₂ ounces jellyfish
    ¹/₂ spiced pork tongue
    2 cucumbers
    1 ounce coriander

Seasoning:
    2 teaspoons sugar
    1 tablespoon vinegar

Sauces for Dipping:
    strange-flavor sauce
    five-flavor sauce
    mustard
    minced garlic and soy sauce

Method:
1. Cook the prawns and the squid. Shell cooked prawns.
2. Soak jellyfish in water till expanded. Slice the jellyfish and marinate it with Seasoning.
3. Slice spiced pork tongue, prawns, squid, and cucumber thinly. Arrange all slices on a plate in a peach shape. Garnish with coriander.
4. Serve with the four sauces for dipping.

Notes:
1. Sauces for dipping are changeable according to your taste.
2. Arranging food in the shape of animals or auspicious things is the creation of Szechuanese. Almost every family has a dish like this in the Chinese New Year or festivals. Besides being auspicious, the dish is also used as an item of competition.
3. Other ways of serving this assorted cold plate are The Butterfly Plate, The Mandarin Duck Plate, The Dragon and Phoenix Plate, The White Crane Plate, and The Peacock Plate.

五福大拼
Wu-Fu Assorted Plate

Ingredients:
5 ounces small shrimps
5 ounces jellyfish head
5 ounces squid
5 ounces pork kidney
5 ounces spiced beef shank
coriander leaves
lettuce
5 cherries

Seasoning (1):
$^1/_2$ tablespoon wine
$^1/_2$ tablespoon soy sauce
$^1/_2$ teaspoon salt
$^1/_2$ teaspoon sugar

Seasoning (2):
1 teaspoon sugar

$^1/_2$ tablespoon soy sauce
sesame oil
MSG

Sauces for Dipping:
mayonnaise
bon-bon sauce
minced ginger and vinegar
minced peppercorn and sesame oil
minced spring onion and soy sauce

Method:
1. Rinse the shrimps and drain well. Remove the dark digestive cord from shrimps. Stir-fry quickly over a high flame with little oil. Add Seasoning (1) and mix well. Stir-fry till there's not much juice left. Remove.
2. Soak jellyfish head in water till soft. Cut into wide strips. Mix the strips with Seasoning (2). Rinse the squid. Remove intestinal canal from squid. Score to make a crisscross pattern. Cook in boiling water till done. Soak pork kidney in water for a while. Slice thinly. Cook in boiling water till done. Slice spiced beef shank thinly.
3. Arrange the five major ingredients on a plate and garnish with coriander leaves, lettuce, and cherries.
4. Serve with the five sauces for dipping.

Notes:
1. Bon-bon sauce is made by mixing sesame sauce, soy sauce, MSG, salt, sugar, minced garlic, sesame oil, and stock. The proportions are adjustable according to your taste.
2. Spiced beef shank is cooked with soy sauce and some spices.

金魚蝦片
Goldfish Prawns Salad

Ingredients:
    12 prawns
    4-5 dried black mushrooms
    1 large carrot
    6 mung bean cakes
    1 cherry
    lettuce

Sauces for Dipping:
    strange-flavor sauce
    minced ginger and soy sauce
    mayonnaise
    mustard and soy sauce

Method:
1. Boil prawns in water till cooked. Shell the cooked prawns. Slice each prawn into four pieces. Soak dried black mushrooms in water till soft. Cut off the stalks. Fry slightly in hot oil. Drain well. Cut a 2″ section of carrot and carve into the shape of a fish mouth. Slice the rest into $1/4$″-thick pieces. Shred the mung bean cakes.
2. Arrange the 3 largest pieces of carrot to make a fish tail. Pile the shreds of mung bean cakes in the middle as a base. Arrange the middle two pieces (the white pieces) of each prawn to form the fish belly. Arrange the black mushrooms to make the two side pieces and use the red pieces of each prawn to form the fish head. Overlap black mushrooms and cherries to make fish eyes. Add the carved-carrot fish mouth. Garnish with lettuce.
3. Serve with the four sauces for dipping.

Notes:
1. When boiling the prawns, boil them with ginger slices, salt, and some wine. Soak the cooked prawns in ice water if they are not to be used immediately.
2. When arranging those slices to make goldfish, remember to start from the tail. This will help you control the pose of the fish.

陳皮牛肉

Stir-Fried Beef with Dried Orange Peel

Ingredients:
- 20 ounces beef
- 6 cups oil for frying
- 2 tablespoons stock
- 2 tablespoons fermented rice
- 1 teaspoon vinegar
- $^1/_2$ teaspoon sesame oil

Seasoning (1):
- 4 ounces dried orange peel
- 4 ounces dried chili
- 20 peppercorns

Seasoning (2):
- 1 teaspoon salt
- $^1/_2$ teaspoon sugar
- $^1/_2$ teaspoon MSG
- 1 tablespoon wine

Method:
1. Slice beef thinly into pieces $1^1/_2'' \times 1^1/_2''$. Marinate with $^1/_2$ teaspoon salt for 20 minutes.
2. Heat oil for frying till over medium hot. Fry beef slices till half cooked. Remove and drain well.
3. Leave a little oil in the wok. Stir-fry Seasoning (1) for a while. Add beef slices, stock, and fermented rice. Add Seasoning (2). Mix well. Stir-fry till there's not much juice left. Add vinegar and sesame oil. Mix well. Remove and serve.

Notes:
1. Choose beef suitable for stir-frying, such as fillet.
2. This is a delicious dish to go with wine. Its taste can be best tasted when chewing slowly.
3. Dried orange peel is slightly bitter and hot.

罈子肉
Beef Brisket in Jar

Ingredients:

    20 ounces beef brisket
    2½ ounces ginger
    5 carrot balls
    5 turnip balls
    1 tablespoon black dates
    1 tablespoon lotus seeds
    2 tablespoons red tomato sauce
    2 teaspoons salt
    1 teaspoon MSG
    4 cups stock
    1 cup Shao-Hsing wine or sherry

Method:

1. Rinse brisket. Cut into 1″ cubes. Cook the cubes in boiling water for a while. Remove and drain well. Pat ginger flat. Cut into 2 pieces.
2. Put the brisket and all other ingredients in a small earthen jar. Seal the jar with mud. Simmer over a low flame for 10 hours. Serve in the jar.
3. If you want to serve it in a soup bowl, let it get cold first, then ladle the brisket out carefully. Steam it in the soup bowl. Serve. If you ladle the brisket out when it is still hot, it will become mashed because it is too well cooked.

Note:

This method can also be used to cook chicken, pork, fish, etc.

麻辣牛筋

Hot and Spicy Beef Tendon

Ingredients:

> 5 ounces beef tendon
> 2 spring onions

Seasoning:

> $1/2$ teaspoon each salt, MSG, sugar, vinegar, ground pepper, and chili oil

Method:

1. Slice the cooked beef tendon and spring onion on a slant.
2. Mix beef tendon slices with spring onion slices and seasoning. Serve.

辣牛肉
Hot Beef

Ingredients:

      10 ounces beef shank
      5 spring onions
      5 slices ginger
      1 tablespoon wine
      $1/2$ tablespoon soy sauce
      $1/2$ teaspoon MSG
      4 chilies
      10 peppercorns and star anise
      $1/2$ teaspoon chili oil

Method:

1. Marinate beef shank with 2 spring onions (sectioned), 1 slice ginger, and $1/2$ tablespoon wine for 30 minutes. Cook the shank in boiling water for a while. Remove and drain well.
2. Mix some water with the remaining spring onions, ginger, and wine, and soy sauce, MSG, chilies, peppercorns, and star anise to make juice.
3. Put the scalded shank in the juice and cook over a low flame for 40 minutes. Remove and drain well. Slice thinly. Pour chili oil on top and serve.

罐煨牛筋

Simmered Beef Tendon in Jar

Ingredients:

        20 ounces beef tendon
        4-5 dried black mushrooms
        2 small bamboo shoots
        2 tablespoons black dates
        2 tablespoons medlars
        2 tablespoons lotus seeds
        2-3 slices licorice
        1 tablespoon dried small shrimps
        5-6 slices ham
        1 tablespoon wine
        1 teaspoon salt
        1 teaspoon MSG
        6 cups stock

Method:

1. Remove fat parts from beef tendon. Cut into 1″ cubes. Cook briefly in boiling water. Soak dried black mushrooms in water till soft. Remove stalks. Cut each mushroom in half. Rinse bamboo shoots. Peel them. Slice thinly. Rinse the black dates, the medlars, and the lotus seeds.
2. Put all ingredients in a flameproof earthen jar. Bring to a boil over a high flame. Switch to a low flame to simmer for 3-4 hours. Serve when the tendon is very soft.

Note:

This dish has a strong Chinese medicine taste. This taste can be reduced by using less of the medlars and licorice and more wine.

青椒牛肉絲

Stir-Fried Beef Shreds with Green Peppers

Ingredients:

        8 ounces beef
        2 large green peppers
        2 chilies
        3 cups vegetable oil
        1 tablespoon ginger shreds
        1/2 teaspoon MSG
        1 tablespoon soy sauce

Seasoning:

        1 egg white
        1/2 teaspoon salt
        1 teaspoon wine
        1/2 teaspoon MSG
        1/2 teaspoon sugar
        1 tablespoon cornstarch

Method:

1. Shred the beef. Marinate with Seasoning for 20 minutes. Rinse green peppers. Seed them. Shred thinly. Rinse chilies. Seed them. Remove stalks and shred thinly.
2. Heat vegetable oil in a wok till hot. Stir-fry the beef shreds quickly till color changes and the shreds become loose. Remove and drain.
3. Save some oil in the wok. Stir-fry quickly the chili shreds and the ginger shreds. Add beef shreds, MSG, and soy sauce. Stir-fry for a while. Add green pepper shreds. Mix well. Serve.

魚香牛肉絲
Stir-Fried Beef Shreds with Fish-Flavored Sauce

Ingredients:

    8 ounces beef
    several water chestnuts
    3 cups oil
    1 tablespoon minced spring onion
    1 tablespoon minced ginger
    1 tablespoon minced garlic
    1 tablespoon hot bean sauce

Seasoning (1):

    1 tablespoon soy sauce
    cornstarch

Seasoning (2):

    1/2 teaspoon salt
    1 teaspoon sugar
    1/2 tablespoon soy sauce
    1 tablespoon dark vinegar
    pepper powder
    1 tablespoon cornstarch paste
    1 teaspoon sesame oil

Method:

1. Rinse beef. Shred it thinly. Marinate with Seasoning (1) for 10 minutes. Rinse water chestnuts. Peel and dice. Mix all ingredients in Seasoning (2) well.
2. Heat oil in a wok till hot. Quickly stir-fry the beef shreds till the beef turns white. Remove and drain.
3. Save some oil in the wok. Stir-fry spring onion, ginger, and garlic for a few seconds. Add water chestnut dice and hot bean sauce. Stir-fry for a while. Add the beef shreds. Mix well. Pour in Seasoning (2). Stir till it turns pasty. Remove and serve.

家常牛肉絲
Beef Shreds, Family Style

Ingredients:

    8 ounces beef
    3-4 celery stalks
    3 cups oil
    1 tablespoon ginger shreds
    1 tablespoon chili shreds
    1 tablespoon hot bean sauce
    1/2 tablespoon soy sauce
    1/2 teaspoon MSG
    1 teaspoon salt
    1 tablespoon wine
    1 teaspoon sesame oil
    1 teaspoon vinegar
    ground pepper

Seasoning:

    1 tablespoon soy sauce
    oyster sauce
    bicarbonate

Method:

1. Rinse beef. Shred it. Marinate with Seasoning for 10 minutes. Rinse celery. Remove the root parts and leaves. Cut into 1"-long sections.
2. Heat oil in a wok. Stir-fry beef shreds quickly till the beef turns white. Remove and drain.
3. Save some oil in the wok. Stir-fry ginger shreds and chili shreds for a few seconds. Add celery. Stir-fry till the celery is half cooked. Add beef shreds, hot bean sauce, soy sauce, MSG, and salt. Mix well. Add wine, sesame oil, and vinegar. Stir-fry for a while. Remove. Sprinkle ground pepper on top. Serve.

Notes:

1. Beef will taste more tender after being marinated with Seasoning. Bicarbonate can be replaced by tenderizer.
2. Celery can be replaced by green pepper shreds. Add them after the beef shreds are cooked, or they will become too soft.

原籠牛肉
Steamed Beef

Ingredients:
    20 ounces beef
    2 sweet potatoes
    cold stock
    1 cup bread crumbs
    sesame oil
    2 tablespoons minced spring onion

Seasoning (1):
    1 tablespoon bean sauce
    1 tablespoon sweet bean sauce
    1 tablespoon soy sauce
    1 teaspoon sugar
    1 teaspoon MSG
    vegetable oil
    minced ginger

Seasoning (2):
    1 tablespoon minced coriander
    2 teaspoons ground pepper
    2 teaspoons minced spring onion

Method:
1. Rinse beef. Slice it thinly. Rinse sweet potatoes. Peel and cut into large cubes.
2. Mix all ingredients in Seasoning (1) well. Marinate beef slices with Seasoning (1) for 20 minutes. Add stock to wet beef. Coat each slice with bread crumbs.
3. Soak sweet potato cubes in the remaining Seasoning (1) for a while. Spread them on the bottom of a small bamboo steamer. Put beef slices on top. Steam over a high flame for 40 minutes.
4. Heat sesame oil. Add minced spring onion. Pour it on top of the steamed beef slices. Serve with Seasoning (2) as a dip.

Notes:
1. Choose lean beef or the part suitable for frying.
2. Remember to slice the beef thinly so that the seasoning can penetrate the whole piece. The above method can also be used to cook chicken, pork, fish, etc.
3. Sweet potato can be replaced by potato, pumpkin, string beans, or snow peas.

螞蟻上樹
Ants Climbing Trees

Ingredients:

  2 packs bean threads (silk noodles)
  4 tablespoons oil
  1 tablespoon minced spring onion
  1 tablespoon minced ginger
  3 ounces ground pork
  1 tablespoon hot bean sauce
  $^1/_2$ cup stock
  1 tablespoon soy sauce
  1 teaspoon salt
  $^1/_2$ teaspoon MSG
  1 tablespoon minced celery
  sesame oil

Method:

1. Soak bean threads in warm water till soft.
2. Heat oil in a wok. Stir-fry spring onion and ginger for a few seconds. Add ground pork and hot bean sauce. Mix well. Pour stock in. Add soy sauce, salt, and MSG.
3. Bring to a boil. Add bean threads and cook till transparent. Add minced celery and minced spring onion. Mix well. Remove.
4. Pour some sesame oil on top. Serve.

Notes:

1. It is best if the pork is very finely ground. Chop it after it is ground, if necessary.
2. Bean threads will turn sticky if there is too much water. Therefore, remember not to leave too much juice.
3. The original way of preparing Ants Climbing Trees is to fry the bean threads till brown first, then cook with stock till soft. But usually the frying step is omitted, because it is very hard to fry bean threads properly.

紅燒牛腩
Stewed Beef Brisket

Ingredients:

  20 ounces beef brisket
  3 tablespoons oil
  3 spring onions (sectioned)
  1 tablespoon ginger shreds
  1 tablespoon minced garlic
  $^1/_2$ cup soy sauce
  1 teaspoon sugar
  3 tablespoons wine
  3-5 star anise
  10 carrot balls
  1 teaspoon sugar color
  1 tablespoon cornstarch paste
  Chinese greens

Method:

1. Rinse the brisket. Put it in a pot and cover it with water. Simmer over a low flame for $1^1/_2$ hours. Remove and drain well. Cut into 1″ cubes. Reserve 1 cup stock.
2. Heat oil in a wok. Stir-fry spring onions, ginger, and garlic for a few seconds. Add soy sauce, sugar, wine, and star anise. Mix well. Add the beef brisket cubes and the stock. Bring to a boil. Lower the flame and simmer for 20 minutes with the cover on.
3. Ladle the brisket cubes out. Arrange them in a plate. Add carrot balls to the juice left in the wok and cook. Add sugar color and cornstarch paste. Pour over the brisket.
4. Boil the Chinese greens till cooked. Tear to pieces. Garnish the plate with the cooked greens.

Note:
See note 1 on p. 47 for how to prepare sugar color.

麻辣燙
Ma-La-Tang (The Hot and Spicy Dish)

Ingredients:

    3 tender bean curds
    1 ounce beef
    3 garlic sprouts
    1 cup oil
    2 teaspoons minced spring onion
    2 teaspoons minced garlic
    1 tablespoon cornstarch paste

Seasoning:

    1 teaspoon hot fermented beans
    1 tablespoon ground pepper
    1 tablespoon chili powder
    1/2 teaspoon salt
    1/2 teaspoon MSG

Method:

1. Remove the hard skin and edge from bean curds. Dice. Cut beef into small cubes. Chop garlic sprouts.
2. Crushed hot fermented beans. Mix with ground pepper.
3. Cook bean curd dice in boiling water for a while. Remove and drain well.
4. Heat oil in a wok till hot. Stir-fry spring onion and garlic for a few seconds. Add the beef dice. Stir-fry till half done. Add bean curd dice and Seasoning. Mix well.
5. Bring to a boil. Add chopped garlic sprouts. Add cornstarch paste. Remove and serve.

Note:

The name "Ma-La-Tang" means that a lot of pepper and chili powder has to be added to make the dish hot and spicy.

魚香芒排
Pork Ribs in Fish-Flavored Sauce

Ingredients:

    3 pounds pork ribs
    6 cups oil
    1 tablespoon soy sauce
    2 teaspoons sugar color
    1 tablespoon MSG
    1 tablespoon cornstarch paste
    3 spring onions

Seasoning:

    3 teaspoons salt
    2 egg whites
    2 tablespoons cornstarch

Method:

1. Chop pork ribs into 4"-long sections. Marinate with Seasoning for 20 minutes.
2. Heat oil in a wok till hot. Fry the ribs till golden brown. Ladle out and drain well.
3. Put the fried ribs in a large bowl. Steam for 15 minutes.
4. Pour the juice into the large bowl after steaming in a wok. Add soy sauce, sugar color, and MSG. Mix well. Add the ribs. Stir-fry for a while. Remove ribs to a plate. Add cornstarch paste to the juice remaining in the wok. Pour the paste over the ribs.
5. Cut the green parts of the spring onions into 4"-long sections. Use to garnish the plate. Serve.

Note:

See note 1 on p. 47 for how to prepare sugar color.

蒜泥白肉
Minced Garlic with White Pork

Ingredients:

    10 ounces pork belly
    3 slices ginger
    2 spring onions (sectioned)
    coriander

Seasoning:

    2 tablespoons minced garlic
    2 tablespoons thick soy sauce
    salt
    MSG
    1 tablespoon cold stock
    $^1/_2$ tablespoon chili oil

Method:

1. Cut off the skin from pork. Rinse. Boil with ginger and spring onions for about 30 minutes. Stick a chopstick into the pork. If there's no more blood coming out of the hole, remove. Cut into thin 2″ × 2″ slices after cools off.
2. Put the pork slices in a strainer. Cook the slices in boiling water for a while. Remove and drain. Arrange the slices on a plate.
3. Mix all ingredients in Seasoning well. Pour it over the pork slices. Chop coriander. Sprinkle the chopped coriander on top of pork slices. Serve.

酥烤大方
Bar-B-Qued Crispy Pork Ribs

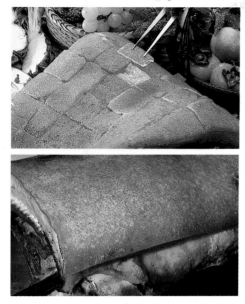

Ingredients:

    2 pounds pork ribs
    2 teaspoons oil
    4 tablespoons sweet flour sauce
    2 teaspoons salt
    1 tablespoon peppercorns
    2 tablespoons natural salt
    1 tablespoon minced spring onion
    1 cup sesame oil
    15 lotus pancakes
    3 pounds large spring onion sections

Method:

1. Trim the pork ribs into a large square. Scrape hair off the skin. Rinse.
2. Put oil in a wok to heat. Add sweet flour sauce and salt. Mix well. Remove.
3. Mix peppercorns and the natural salt together. Fry them in a pan without oil till it smells good. Mix with minced spring onion after it cools off. Spread evenly on the pork ribs. Let stand for a while.

4. Stick a steel fork into the pork ribs. Keep the fork as close to the bone as possible. Pierce the side closer to the bones to make some small holes so that oil can leak out through these holes during roasting.
5. Brush sesame oil on the pork skin. Roast, skin side first, over a high flame till it turns scorched and black. Remove. Cover the skin with a piece of clean, wet cloth.
6. Remove the cloth after the skin gets soft. Scrape off the black shell. Brush sesame oil on it. Roast over a medium flame. Roast the bone side first till it turns golden brown. Turn it over and roast the skin side till it is scorched. Remove.
7. Scrape off the scorched parts from the skin. Brush some sesame oil on it. Roast the skin side over a small flame till it turns golden brown and crispy. Remove.
8. Put the pork ribs on a large plate. Score the skin side to make a crisscross pattern, with each square about 2″×2″. Serve with lotus pancakes, sweet flour sauce, and large spring onion sections.

Notes:

1. Crispy and nongreasy taste is the characteristic of this dish. When having this dish, wrap a piece of the skin and some spring onion with a piece of lotus pancake coated with sweet flour sauce.
2. The official way of having this dish is that, after the skin part is eaten up, the remaining meat and ribs are carried back to the kitchen, to be processed again. The fillet part is used in the dish Minced Garlic with White Pork and served together with four other plates-Pickled Cucumber, String Beans in Ginger and Vinegar, Hot and Spicy Bean Curd Skin, and Pickled Mustard Stem. The brisket part is made into Double-Cooked Pork and served with Steamed Shredded Rolls. The ribs are chopped into large cubes to make Sweet and Sour Ribs, Ribs with Pepper and Salt, or Ribs with Fish-Flavored Sauce. Only when the fourth and last dish is served can this Bar-B-Qued Crispy Pork Ribs be considered completely eaten up. That is why this dish is also named Bar-B-Qued Crispy Pork Prepared in Four Different Ways.

京醬肉絲

Stir-Fried Pork Shreds with Sweet Flour Sauce

Ingredients:

    8 ounces pork
    5 spring onions
    3 cups oil
    3 tablespoons sweet flour sauce
    1 teaspoon salt
    $\frac{1}{2}$ teaspoon sugar
    1 teaspoon MSG
    1 tablespoon stock

Seasoning:

    1 tablespoon wine
    1 teaspoon salt
    1 tablespoon cornstarch

Method:

1. Shred the pork thinly. Marinate with Seasoning for 20 minutes. Shred spring onions.
2. Heat oil in a wok. Stir-fry spring onion shreds briefly. Remove. Drain well. Spread evenly on a plate. Stir-fry pork shreds till they turn loose and the color changes. Remove and drain.
3. Save some oil in the wok. Add sweet flour sauce, salt, sugar, and MSG. Stir-fry. Add pork shreds and stock. Mix well. Remove when the pork is completely done. Remove and pour over the spring onion shreds. Serve.

回鍋肉
Double-Cooked Pork

Ingredients:

    8 ounces pork
    2 green peppers (large)
    2 garlic sprouts
    3 tablespoons oil
    2 tablespoons sweet flour sauce
    1 tablespoon hot bean sauce
    1 teaspoon stock
    1 teaspoon sugar
    $1/2$ teaspoon MSG

Method:

1. Rinse the pork. Put it in cold water. Boil over a high flame for 20 minutes. Stick a chopstick into the pork; if there's no more blood coming out from it, remove. Slice thinly after it cools off.

2. Rinse green peppers. Seed and remove ribs. Cut into 1″ squares. Remove old and dry parts from garlic sprouts. Section.

3. Heat oil in a wok. Stir-fry pork slices till the fat part shrinks. Add green peppers. Stir-fry for a while. Remove.

4. Add Sweet flour sauce and hot bean sauce to the oil remaining in the wok. Stir for a while. Add stock, sugar, and MSG. Mix well. Pour the pork slices and green peppers back and stir-fry for a while. Add the garlic sprouts. Stir-fry briefly. Remove and serve.

火爆双脆

Stir-Fried Pork Kidney with Duck Giblets

Ingredients:
2 duck giblets (gizzards, livers, and hearts)
1 pork kidney
1 ounce snow peas
5 cups oil
5 slices ginger
2 spring onions
1 tablespoon wine
sesame oil

Seasoning:
1 tablespoon ginger wine
1 1/2 teaspoons salt
1/2 teaspoon MSG
1 teaspoon ground pepper
1 tablespoon cornstarch

Method:
1. Rinse the duck gizzards, livers, and hearts. Slice. Rinse pork kidney. Slice. Score each slice to make a crisscross pattern. Marinate the duck giblets and the pork kidney with Seasoning for 10 minutes. Remove stems and the hard edges from the snow peas. Rinse.
2. Heat oil in a wok. Fry the giblets and the kidney briefly. Remove and drain.
3. Save some oil in the wok. Quickly stir-fry ginger and spring onions. Add the giblets and kidney. Mix well. when almost done, add wine and snow peas. Stir-fry quickly. Remove.
4. Drip sesame oil on top. Serve.

Note:
Chicken gizzard and squid can be used to replace duck giblets and pork kidney.

桂花蹄筋
Osmanthus Sinew

Ingredients:

3 ounces pork sinew (already soaked in water)
3 cups stock
$\frac{1}{2}$ teaspoon salt
$\frac{1}{2}$ teaspoon MSG
1 teaspoon minced chicken meat
2 teaspoons milk
2 tablespoons cold stock
$\frac{1}{2}$ teaspoon cornstarch
2 teaspoons each minced green pepper, minced dried small shrimps, and minced ham
4 egg whites
3 tablespoons lard
chicken oil (rendered chicken fat)

Method:

1. Cut the sinew into $1\frac{1}{2}$"-long strips. Scald in boiling water briefly. Add the stock with some salt and MSG and boil for a while. Remove and drain.
2. Mix the minced chicken meat with milk, cold stock, cornstarch, minced green pepper, 1 teaspoon minced dried small shrimps, minced ham, salt, and MSG. Mix well.
3. Beat egg whites until stiff. Combine with the mixture above.
4. Heat lard in a preheated wok. Pour the mixture in. Stir-fry over a low flame till almost done. Add sinew. Stir-fry till cooked.
5. Remove. Sprinkle on the remaining minced dried small shrimps and drip some chicken oil on top. Serve.

Notes:

1. The wok should be preheated so that the mixture won't stick to it. The dish taste even better with lard used instead of oil.
2. This dish should be served and eaten immediately after it is removed from the wok. It is a good dish in the winter.

東坡金腳
Tung-Po Golden Pork Feet

Ingredients:

    1 pork foot
    soy sauce
    6 cups oil for frying
    2 cups stock
    2 teaspoons dried pickled cabbage
    2 teaspoons sesame oil
    1 tablespoon cornstarch paste
    1 tablespoon minced spring onion
    10 each of carrot and turnip balls

Seasoning:

    5 slices ginger
    peppercorns
    1 teaspoon ground pepper
    1 tablespoon soy sauce
    2 teaspoons salt
    1 tablespoon MSG
    1 teaspoon sugar color
    $1/2$ tablespoon wine

Method:

1. Scrape hair off the pork foot. Rinse. Chop into sections. Remove bones. Cook in boiling water briefly. Add some soy sauce to the pork foot.
2. Heat oil for frying. Fry the pork foot till golden brown. Remove and drain.
3. Save some oil in the wok. Add Seasoning. Stir quickly. Add stock and pork foot. Simmer over a low flame for 1 hour. Remove. Steam for 10 minutes.
4. Save the juice oozing out from the pork foot. Put the pork foot, upside down, in the plate.
5. Stir-fry the dried pickled cabbage with sesame oil. Add the juice above, cornstarch paste, and spring onion. Mix well. Pour it over the pork foot.
6. Fry the carrot and the turnip balls for 3 minutes. Garnish the dish with them and the spinach. Serve.

Notes:

1. Sugar color is made by frying granulated sugar and rock sugar with oil over very a small flame. It looks like thick soy sauce and helps deepen the color of the dish.
2. The dish is called Tung-Po Golden Pork Feet because its preparation is like that of Tung-Po Pork.

"Portrait of Su Tung-Po"
Collection of the National Palace Museum

粉蒸肥腸
Steamed Bread-Crumb-Coated Pork Intestine

Ingredients:
10 ounces large pork intestine
1 cup bread crumbs
3 ounces peeled sweet potato
1 teaspoon sesame oil
minced spring onion
ground pepper

Seasoning:
1 tablespoon soy sauce
$^1/_2$ tablespoon hot bean sauce
1 tablespoon wine
$^1/_2$ teaspoon sugar
$^1/_2$ tablespoon sweet flour sauce
$^1/_2$ teaspoon MSG
$^1/_2$ teaspoon ground pepper
$^1/_2$ teaspoon minced ginger
$^1/_2$ teaspoon minced spring onion

Method:
1. Rinse pork intestine. Cut into $^3/_4$"-long sections. Marinate with Seasoning for 20 minutes. Mix with the bread crumbs.
2. Cut sweet potato into cubes. Mix with the remaining juice from marinating the intestine. Spread evenly on the bottom of each steamer. Put the intestine sections evenly on top of the sweet potato.
3. Steam over a high flame for 1 hour.
4. Drip some hot sesame oil on top. Sprinkle some minced spring onion and ground pepper on top and serve.

麻婆腦花
Ma-Po's Pork Brain

Ingredients:
- 3 pork brains
- 2 tablespoons oil
- 4 ounces ground pork
- 2 cups stock
- 1 tablespoon cornstarch paste

Seasoning (1):
- 2 tablespoons hot bean sauce
- 1 teaspoon minced ginger

Seasoning (2):
- $1/2$ tablespoon soy sauce
- $1/2$ teaspoon MSG
- 1 teaspoon wine

Seasoning (3):
- $1/2$ teaspoon sesame oil
- 1 teaspoon minced spring onion
- 1 teaspoon ground pepper

Method:
1. Cook pork brains in boiling water till done. Remove membrane and tissue. Cut into long, thin slices.
2. Heat oil in a wok. Stir-fry ground pork with Seasoning (1) till the ground pork turns crispy. Add stock, the pork brains, and Seasoning (2). Simmer over a low flame till there's almost no juice left. Add cornstarch paste. Remove.
3. Sprinkle Seasoning (3) on top and serve.

Note:
Besides pork brains, beef brains can also be cooked this way.

東腸旺

...Pork Intestine over
...-Ching Burner

...tine
...ck blood curd
...e

...ut
...ns oil
...er
...c
... hot bean sauce
...eppercorns
...alt
...ugar

... cornstarch paste
...sesame oil

...estine. Rub with salt to clean. Rinse
...lood curd and sour cabbage into 1″
... chilies and the garlic sprout.
... in boiling water for a while. Cut
...ons. Put it in a small pot with duck
...ur cabbage.
...Stir-fry ginger, garlic, and hot bean
..., peppercorns, salt, sugar, and
...oil. Add cornstarch paste. Pour it
...Add garlic sprout and simmer for
...over the Wu-Ching burner.
...oil on top before serving.

荷葉排骨

Steamed Pork Ribs Wrapped
in Lotus Leaves

Ingredients:

    12 ounces pork ribs
    3 teaspoons salt
    3 tablespoons soy sauce
    3 tablespoons wine
    2 large lotus leaves
    2 tablespoons Wu-Hsiang (Five-Flavored) powder
    1 cup bread crumbs

Method:

1. Chop pork ribs into 4″-long section. Marinate with salt, soy sauce, and wine for 3 hours.
2. Remove hard stem from lotus leaves. Divide each piece into 3 small pieces. Cook briefly in boiling water to make them soft.
3. Mix wu-hsiang powder and bread crumbs. Coat each section of the marinated ribs with the mixture.
4. Wrap one section of ribs with one piece of lotus leaf. Arrange the packets in a plate. Steam over a high flame for 2-3 hours.
5. Serve while it is still hot. It smells wonderful because of the lotus leaf. The meat is very tender.

Note:
Either fresh or dried lotus leaf can be used.

樟茶鴨
Chang-Cha Duck (Smoked Duck)

Ingredients:
- 1 duck (about 4 pounds)
- 8 cups oil

Seasoning (1):
- 1 tablespoon peppercorns
- 3 tablespoons salt
- 1 teaspoon saltpeter powder

Seasoning (2):
- 2 cups crumbs of camphor wood
- 1 tablespoon dried orange peel
- 1 tablespoon peppercorns
- 1 tablespoon star anise
- 1 teaspoon saltpeter powder
- 1 teaspoon sugar

Method:
1. Fry the peppercorns and salt of Seasoning (1) in a clean, dry pan. Crush the mixture after it turns cold. Mix with saltpeter powder.
2. Remove internal organs from the duck. Rinse. Remove all feathers. Rub Seasoning (1) all over the duck. Let stand for 6-8 hours.
3. Wipe Seaosning (1) off the duck. Hang it in a windy and dry place for 6 hours.
4. Put Seasoning (2) in a wok. Set a rack in the wok. Put the duck on it. Cover the wok. Put it on a stove. Bake over a low flame. Turn the duck upside down every 10 minutes. Bake till it turns tea brown. Remove.
5. Steam the duck for 2 hours over a high flame.
6. Heat oil in a wok till very hot. Fry the duck till its skin turns golden brown and crispy. Remove and drain. Chop into 1″×2″ pieces while it is still hot. Arrange them neatly on a plate. Garnish with coriander, carved vegetable, or fruit.
7. Serve with large spring onion sections and sweet flour sauce.

Note:
The duck tastes wonderful, with crispy skin and tender meat, it is a highly welcomed dish in a Szechuanese banquet.

Crispy Duck S

Ingredients:

1 already-made crispy d
3 tablespoons minced h
4 ounces duck breast m
6 cups oil
cornstarch
1 tablespoon mixed p

Seasoning:

2 tablespoon
1 teaspoon
1/2 teaspoo

Method:

1. Remove bones
   to shreds. Place
   a layer of mince

2. Mince the duck
   Pour it into the t
   all the duck shre

3. Put the tray in a s
   20 minutes. Rea
   1" × 2" pieces.

4. Heat oil in a wo
   with cornstarch.
   drain.

5. Garnish with co
   base. Arrange
   peppersalt.

Note:

The easier way o
whole duck instea
the preparation is t

怪味雞塊
Strange-Flavored Chicken Pieces

Ingredients:
  1 tender chicken
  lettuce
  coriander

Seasoning:
  1 teaspoon minced ginger
  1 teaspoon minced garlic
  3 tablespoons thick soy sauce
  1 teaspoon sugar
  $1/2$ tablespoon vinegar
  2 teaspoons sesame sauce
  1 teaspoon ground pepper
  MSG
  2 teaspoons chili oil

Method:
1. Rinse chicken. Remove its internal organs. Cook it in boiling water till done. Soak in ice water till it cools off completely.
2. Drain chicken well. Cut off head, legs, and claws. Chop into $2'' \times 1''$ pieces. Arrange them on a plate.
3. Mix Seasoning well to make strange-flavored sauce. Pour it over chicken pieces. Garnish with lettuce and coriander. Serve.

Notes:
1. The original taste of the chicken is preserved by the soaking in ice water right after it is removed from the boiling water. The meat will be tender this way.
2. Strange-flavored sauce tastes sour, salty, hot, spicy, and sweet at the same time, but its taste is far from strange. This is a very delicious dish. In the summer, the dish can be served as a cold plate.

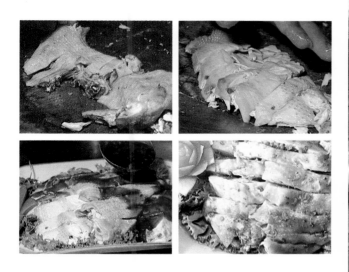

碎米雞丁
Stir-Fried Chicken Dice with Peanuts

Ingredients:

8 ounces chicken breast
$^1/_2$ cabbage
2 tablespoons fried peanuts
2 chilies
5 cups oil
1 tablespoon hot bean sauce
2 teaspoons salt
1 teaspoon MSG

Method:

1. Slice chicken breast on a slant. Pat with the flat side of the chopper. Dice.
2. Rinse cabbage. Remove hard stem. Cut into $^3/_8''$ squares. Remove skin from the fried peanuts. Crush to small granules. Rinse chilies. Mince.
3. Heat oil in a wok. Fry chicken dice and cabbage dice briefly. Remove when color of the pork changes.
4. Save 3 tablespoons oil in the wok. Stir-fry hot bean sauce first for a while. Add chicken dice and cabbage. Mix well. Add the peanut granules, minced chilies, salt and MSG. Stir-fry well. Remove and serve.

Notes:

1. Szechuanese pickled cabbage and chilies can be used to replace cabbage and chilies. This dish will taste even better because of the special flavor of Szechuanese pickles.
2. Peanuts can be replaced by pine seeds if this dish is served at a banquet.

香瓜雞盅
Chicken in Cantaloup Pot

Ingredients:

6 cantaloups

Stuffing:

8 ounces chicken breast
3 eggs
3 dried black mushrooms
3 tablespoons minced ham
4 teaspoons minced ginger
3 teaspoons salt
3 teaspoons MSG
lard
2 tablespoons stock

Method:

1. Rinse cantaloups. Cut off $^3/_4''$ from the stem end. Dig out seeds. Mince chicken breast. Beat eggs well. Soak dried black mushrooms in water till soft. Remove stalks. Mince.
2. Mix all stuffing ingredients well. Pour the mixture into the 6 cantaloups.
3. Put the cantaloup pots in a steamer and steam for 15 minutes. Remove and serve.

Note:

Adding lard to the stuffing makes the minced chicken taste more tender. Minced pork fat can be used to replace lard.

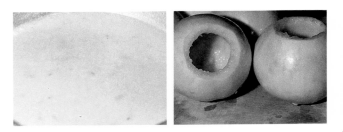

57

宮保雞丁
Kung-Pao Chicken Dice

Ingredients:
- $1/2$ chicken
- 5 cups oil
- 1 tablespoon fried peanuts

Seasoning (1):
- 1 egg white
- 1 teaspoon salt
- 1 tablespoon cornstarch

Seasoning (2):
- 1 ounce dried chili sections
- 1 teaspoon minced garlic

Seasoning (3):
- 1 tablespoon soy sauce
- 1 tablespoon wine
- $1/2$ teaspoon MSG
- 1 teaspoon Sugar
- 1 teaspoon vinegar
- 1 tablespoon cornstarch paste
- 1 teaspoon sesame oil

Method:
1. Remove bones from chicken. Cut into $3/8''$ cubes. Marinate in Seasoning (1).
2. Heat oil in a wok. Fry chicken dice till cooked. Remove and drain.
3. Save some oil in the wok. Stir-fry Seasoning (2) for a while. Add chicken dice. Stir-fry. Add Seasoning (3). Mix well. Add fried peanuts. Stir-fry for a few seconds. Remove and serve.

Notes:
1. Kung-Pao Chicken Dice is a very famous Szechuanese dish. There's an interesting story behind the name of this dish. At the end of the Ching Dynasty, a new governor was assigned to Szechuan Province. To welcome him, the local noblemen arranged a banquet and asked the chef to prepare some new dishes. Among all the new dishes, the dish of chicken dice was the favorite of the new governor. Because the new governor had the position of "Kung-Pao," this dish was thus named Kung-Pao Chicken Dice.
2. Besides providing hot flavor, chilies can also stimulate digestion and increase appetite.

芙蓉雞片
Fu-Yung Chicken Slices

Ingredients:
- 4 ounces chicken breast
- 4 egg whites
- 1 teaspoon bean powder
- 3 cups oil
- 4 ounces lard
- 3 slices ginger
- 3-5 spring onion sections
- 1 cup stock
- 1/2 teaspoon salt
- 1/2 teaspoon MSG
- 1 tablespoon cornstarch paste
- chicken oil (rendered chicken fat)

Seasoning (1):
- salt
- 2 tablespoons milk

Seasoning (2):
- 6 dried black mushrooms
- 1 ounce bamboo shoot slices
- 3 ounces ham slices

Method:
1. Mince chicken breast. Mix with Seasoning (1).
2. Beat egg whites until stiff. Add above mixture and bean powder. Mix well.
3. Heat oil in a wok to over medium hot. Use a teaspoon to ladle out 1 spoonful of the batter and put it in the oil. Repeat. Remove the slices when they turn solid. Drain.
4. Soak dried black mushrooms in water till soft. Remove stalks. Cook all ingredients in Seasoning (2) in boilding water for a while.
5. Put lard in a wok. Stir-fry ginger and spring onion for a few seconds. Add stock and remove ginger and spring onion. Add chicken slices, Seasoning (2), salt, and MSG. Boil till there's almost no juice left. Add cornstarch paste.
6. Drip some chicken oil on top and serve.

Notes:
1. Remember not to use overheated oil to fry chicken slices, or the slices will turn brown and look not so good.
2. Green vegetables can be used to garnish this dish.

成都子雞

Cheng-Du Tender Chicken

Ingredients:

$^1/_2$ tender chicken
$^1/_2$ cup oil
1 tablespoon wine
1 teaspoon minced ginger
1 cup hot stock
1 tablespoon cornstarch paste
1 teaspoon minced spring onion
5 ounces tender pea shoots

Seasoning (1):

1 tablespoon minced red chili
2 tablespoons hot bean sauce

Seasoning (2):

2 teaspoons salt
1 teaspoon sugar

Method:

1. Chop chicken into 1″ squares.
2. Heat oil in a wok. Stir-fry chicken over a high flame for 2 minutes. Add Seasoning (1). Stir-fry for a while. Add wine, minced ginger, and Seasoning (2). Mix well. Add hot stock. Cover the wok and simmer for 5 minutes.
3. Add cornstarch paste. Add minced spring onion. Mix well. Remove and serve.
4. Cook pea shoots in boiling water. Use to garnish the plate.

Note:

Hot bean sauce is made of chilies and beans. The typical Szechuan hot bean sauce is made of fresh chilies and kidney beans.

賞妃雞翅

The Royal Mistress Chicken Wings

Ingredients:
12 chicken wings
2 spring onions
1 cup oil
1 tablespoon granulated rock sugar
5 slices ginger
1 teaspoon salt
$1/2$ teaspoon MSG
3 tablespoons soy sauce
1 cup wine
1 cup stock
10 slices bamboo shoot
1 tablespoon cornstarch
sesame oil

Method:
1. Cut off the ends and joints from chicken wings. Save only the middle sections. Remove all feathers. Rinse. Scald in boiling water for a while. Slice the spring onions.
2. Heat oil in a wok. Add rock sugar. When the melted sugar turns to golden brown, add chicken wings, spring onions, ginger, salt, MSG, and soy sauce. Stir-fry well. Add wine and stock. Simmer over a low flame for 20 minutes.
3. Add bamboo shoot slices. Switch to a high flame and let boil for $1/2$ minute. Where there's almost no juice left, add cornstarch paste. Drip some sesame oil on top. Remove and serve.

Note:
Use a good wine, such as grape wine or Shao-Hsing wine.

大千子雞
Da-Chien Chicken

Ingredients:
2 pounds young cock
3 green peppers
3 red chilies
4 garlic cloves
4 cups oil

Seasoning (1):
1 teaspoon soy sauce
1 egg white
1 teaspoon cornstarch

Seasoning (2):
1 teaspoon soy sauce
$^1/_2$ teaspoon MSG
$^1/_2$ teaspoon sugar
$^1/_2$ teaspoon vinegar
$^1/_2$ teaspoon sugar color
salt
1 teaspoon cornstarch
sesame oil

Method:
1. Rinse chicken. Chop into $^3/_8'' \times 2''$ pieces. Marinate with Seasoning (1).
2. Rinse green peppers and red chilies. Remove seeds and stalks. Cut into pieces around the size of the chicken pieces. Slice garlic.
3. Heat oil in a wok. Fry chicken pieces till cooked. Remove and drain well.
4. Save some oil in the wok. Stir-fry green peppers, red chilies, and garlic for a few seconds. Add chicken pieces and Seasoning (2). Stir-fry quickly. Remove when well mixed. Serve.

Notes:
1. The famous and great painter, the late Mr. Chang Da-Chien, was a gourmet. This dish was first made by a Chinese chef at Tokyo. It's named Da-Chien Chicken because the chef made this dish under the directions of Mr. Chang Da-Chien.
2. See note 1 on p. 47 for how to prepare sugar color.

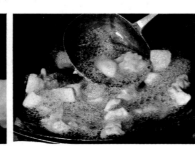

椒麻四件
Four Hot and Spicy Items

Ingredients:
- 3 duck giblets
- 5 wood ears
- 1 bamboo shoot
- 3 ounces white Chinese cabbage
- 10 peppercorns
- 1 teaspoon sesame oil
- 2 teaspoons minced spring onion

Seasoning:
- 2 teaspoons salt
- $1/2$ teaspoon MSG
- 2 teaspoons vinegar

Method:
1. Slice the duck giblets (gizzards, livers, hearts, and intestine) thinly. Rinse wood ears. Slice. Remove skin of bamboo shoot. Slice thinly. Rinse white Chinese cabbage. Section.
2. Cook above ingredients in boiling water till done. Soak in cold boiled water. Drain. Mix with Seasoning.
3. Crush the peppercorns. Mix with minced spring onion and seasame oil. Pour on top of the four items. Serve.

豆辦鯉魚
Carp with Bean Sauce

Ingredients:

    1 carp (medium-size)
    3 tablespoons oil
    1 cup stock
    1 tablespoon cornstarch paste
    minced spring onion
    sesame oil

Seasoning (1):

    1 tablespoon minced ginger
    1 tablespoon minced garlic
    1 tablespoon hot bean sauce
    fermented rice

Seasoning (2):

    $1/2$ teaspoon salt
    $1/2$ teaspoon MSG
    $1/2$ teaspoon sugar
    1 teaspoon vinegar
    1 teaspoon wine

Method:

1. Scrape off the scales from the carp. Remove the guts and the gills. Rinse. Score each side of the fish to make three parallel slanting lines.
2. Heat oil in a wok. Stir-fry Seasoning (1) for a few seconds. Add stock and the carp. Switch to a low flame. Simmer for about 10 minutes. Remove carp from the wok with a pair of chopsticks. Put it in an oval plate.
3. Save the juice in the wok. Add Seasoning (2). Mix well. Add cornstarch paste. Pour over the carp.
4. Sprinkle minced spring onion and sesame oil on top and serve.

乾煸鱔片
Dry-Fried Eel Slices

Ingredients:
    8 ounces eel
    3 pickled chilies
    3 pickled garlic cloves
    3 ounces celery
    6 cups oil
    5 slices pickled ginger
    $1/2$ tablespoon hot bean sauce
    3 tablespoons stock
    ground pepper

Seasoning (1):
    $1/2$ tablespoon soy sauce
    $1/2$ teaspoon MSG
    $1/2$ teaspoon sugar

Seasoning (2):
    $1/2$ teaspoon vinegar

Method:
1. Rinse eel. Cut up. Slice pickled chilies and pickled garlic. Rinse celery. Cut into 2″-long sections.
2. Heat oil to very hot in a wok. Fry eel slices until dry and crispy. Remove and drain.
3. Save some oil in the wok. Stir-fry ginger, garlic, and hot bean sauce for a while. Add eel slices, celery, and Seasoning (1). Stir-fry.
4. When ingredients are well mixed, add stock. Keep boiling till there's not much juice left. Add Seasoning (2). Mix well. Remove. Sprinkle ground pepper on top. Serve.

宮保蝦仁
Kung-Pao Shelled Shrimps

Ingredients:
- 10 ounces shelled shrimps
- 4 cups oil

Seasoning (1):
- 1 egg white
- 2 teaspoons cornstarch
- salt

Seasoning (2):
- ½ tablespoon soy sauce
- 1 teaspoon wine
- ½ teaspoon MSG
- ½ teaspoon sugar
- ½ teaspoon vinegar
- ½ teaspoon sugar color
- cornstarch paste
- sesame oil

Seasoning (3):
- 1 ounce dried chili sections
- minced garlic
- 10 peppercorns

Method:
1. Rinse shelled shrimps. Drain. Marinate with Seasoning (1).
2. Mix all ingredients in Seasoning (2) well.
3. Heat oil in a wok. Fry shrimps over a high flame till they are partly cooked. Remove and drain.
4. Save some oil in the wok. Stir-fry Seasoning (3) for a few seconds. Add the shrimps. Stir-fry till cooked. Add Seasoning (2). Mix well. Remove and serve.

川蒜燒鯰魚
Stewed Sheatfish with Garlic

Ingredients:
- 3 sheatfish
- 1 cup garlic cloves
- 6 tablespoons oil
- 2 teaspoons minced garlic
- 1 tablespoon minced ginger
- 2 tablespoons hot bean sauce
- 2 teaspoons salt
- 1 tablespoon sugar
- 1 tablespoon MSG
- 2 tablespoons soy sauce
- 2 cups stock
- 1 tablespoon minced spring onion
- 1 tablespoon cornstarch paste
- 3 tablespoons vinegar

Method:
1. Rinse sheatfish. Remove the guts and the gills. Cut off fish mouth. Score 4-5 lines on each side of the fish. Peel the garlic cloves. Cut off both ends of each clove.
2. Heat oil in a wok. Stir-fry garlic cloves and minced garlic for a while. Add minced ginger, hot bean sauce, salt, sugar, MSG, and soy sauce. Mix well. Add the sheatfish and stock. Bring to a boil. Lower the flame and simmer for 10-15 minutes. Remember to turn the fish once during simmering.
3. When the fish is well cooked, remove with chopsticks. Save the juice in the wok. Add minced spring onion. Stir for a while. Add cornstarch paste. Add vinegar before removing the sauce from the wok. Pour over the fish. Serve.

First Class Black Sea Cucumbers

Ingredients:

1 spring onion
3 slices ginger
6 black sea cucumbers (already soaked in water)
5 ounces lard
1 tablespoon cornstarch water
1 teaspoon sesame oil
4 ounces green vegetable

Seasoning (1):

1 bamboo shoot
4 dried black mushrooms
1/2 ounce dried small shrimps
1 ounce ham
3 ounces pork stomach
3 ounces chicken meat
1 ounce lotus seeds
1 ounce peas

Seasoning (2):

1 tablespoon soy sauce
1/2 teaspoon salt
2 teaspoons wine
1/2 teaspoons MSG
2 teaspoons ground pepper
1 teaspoon sugar color
1 cup stock

Method:

1. Slice the spring onion. Mince a slice of ginger.
2. Rinse black sea cucumbers. Boil with spring onion sections, water, and ginger slices over a low flame for 5 minutes. Remove and drain. Score the inside of the sea cucumbers to make a crisscross pattern.
3. Peel the bamboo shoot. Soak dried black mushrooms in water till soft. Remove stalks. Dice all the ingredients in Seasoning (1).
4. Put lard in the wok. Stir-fry Seasoning (1) with minced ginger for a while. Add Seasoning (2). Keep boiling till there's no juice left. Remove.
5. Stuff the stir-fried ingredients into the sea cucumbers. Arrange stuffed sea cucumbers in a bowl with the darker side down (the opened side up). Steam for 1 hour.
6. Save the juice in the bowl after steaming. Pour the sea cucumbers out upside down into a plate. Add cornstarch paste to the juice in the wok. Add sesame oil. Pour it on the sea cucumbers. Garnish with some stir-fried green vegetable. Serve.

Notes:

1. Sea cucumbers are very nutritious. They have lots of protein.
2. Sea cucumbers are good for both children and older people, because cooked sea cucumbers are non-greasy, soft, and easy to digest.
3. See the note on p. 99 for how to clean pork stomach.

乾燒明蝦
Broiled Prawns with Tomato and Hot Bean Sauce

Ingredients:
    8 prawns
    $^3/_4$ cup oil
    1 tablespoon minced ginger
    1 tablespoon minced spring onion
    2 tablespoons minced garlic
    4 tablespoons tomato sauce
    1 tablespoon hot bean sauce
    1 tablespoon cornstarch paste

Seasoning:
    1 tablespoon wine
    1 tablespoon salt
    $^1/_2$ teaspoon MSG
    1 tablespoon soy sauce
    1 teaspoon sugar
    3 tablespoons stock

Method:
1. Cut off the prawns barbels and feet. Cut open each prawns back. Remove the black digestive cord.
2. Heat $^1/_4$ cup oil in a pan. Cook the prawns over a low flame. When one side is cooked, turn the prawns over to cook the other side. Remove when the prawns are well done.
3. Put the cooked prawns in water with some minced ginger. Bring to a boil. Remove and drain.
4. Put the remaining oil in a wok. Stir-fry spring onion, ginger, and garlic for a few seconds. Add tomato sauce and hot bean sauce. Mix well. Add seasoning and the prawns. Bring to a boil. Lower the flame and simmer till there's almost no juice left. Add cornstarch paste. Remove and serve.

Note:
The boiling step is necessary to remove the oil attached to the grilled prawns so that the seasoning can be absorbed by the prawns.

豆腐鯉魚
Bean Curd with Carp

Ingredients:
2 bean curds
1 carp
3 cups oil
1 tablespoon minced spring onion
1 tablespoon minced ginger
1 tablespoon minced garlic
1 tablespoon hot bean sauce
2 tablespoons soy sauce
wine
2 teaspoons salt
1 teaspoon MSG
3 cups stock
1 tablespoon cornstarch paste

Method:
1. Cut off the hard edge and skin of the bean curds. Cut into $1^1/_2'' \times ^1/_2''$-long strips. Scrape the scales off the carp. Remove the guts and the gills. Score 3 lines on each side of fish.
2. Heat oil in a wok. Fry bean curd strips to golden brown. Remove and drain. Fry the carp briefly. Remove and drain.
3. Save some oil in the wok. Stir-fry spring onion, ginger, and garlic for a few seconds. Add hot bean sauce. Mix well. Add the carp, bean curd, soy sauce, wine, salt, MSG, and stock. Bring to a boil. Let boil for 5-8 minutes. Remove the fish with chopsticks.
4. Save the juice in the wok. Add cornstarch paste. Pour on top of fish. Serve.

糖醋魚捲
Sweet and Sour Fish Rolls

Ingredients:
    10 ounces yellow fish meat
    3 ounces water chestnuts
    1 egg white
    6 thin bean curd skins
    5 cups oil
    2 teaspoons minced spring onion
    1 teaspoon minced ginger
    2 teaspoons minced garlic

Seasoning (1):
    1 teaspoon salt
    $1/2$ teaspoon MSG
    1 tablespoon wine
    $1/2$ tablespoon ginger juice
    1 tablespoon cornstarch
    oyster sauce

Seasoning (2):
    2 tablespoons tomato sauce
    2 teaspoons sugar
    2 teaspoons vinegar
    $1/2$ teaspoon salt
    $1/2$ teaspoon MSG
    $1/2$ tablespoon cornstarch paste
    1 teaspoon sesame oil

Method:
1. Cut fish meat into $3/8'' \times 2''$-long strips. Marinate with Seasoning (1) for 15 minutes. Shred water chestnuts. Beat egg white well.
2. Wipe bean curd skins clean. Cut each in half to make 12 pieces. Coat one side of each piece with egg white. Wrap 1 tablespoon fish meat and some water chestnut shreds with a piece of bean curd skin to make a $1'' \times 2''$ rectangular roll.
3. Heat oil in a wok to over medium hot. Fry the fish rolls to golden brown. Remove and drain. Arrange on a plate.
4. Save some oil in the wok. Stir-fry spring onion, ginger, and garlic for a few seconds. Add Seasoning (2). Mix well. Pour over the fish rolls. Serve.

Notes:
1. Together with Seasoning (1), Seasoning (2) can also be used to marinate fish meat. Without the sauce made from Seasoning (2), fried fish rolls can be served with pepper and salt.
2. Chicken meat, squid, abalone, etc., can all be cooked this way.

四味鮑片
Four-Flavored Abalone Slices

Ingredients:
- 1 can abalone
- 4 mung bean cakes

Sauces for Dipping:
- strange-flavored sauce
- soy sauce with minced ginger
- soy sauce with mustard
- mayonnaise

Method:
1. Remove abalone from can. Slice thinly. Shred mung bean cakes.
2. Spread mung bean cake shreds evenly on a plate, as a base. Array abalone slices on top. Garnish with carved vegetable or fruit. Serve with the four sauces for dipping.

Note:
Abalone meat has abundant protein and vitamin A. It has been considered a very nutritious food since ancient times.

五更豆酥龍象

Codfish with Szechuanese Fermented Beans over Wu-Ching Burner

Ingredients:

- ½ codfish (about 2 pounds)
- 1 tablespoon wine
- 3 tablespoons oil
- 1 teaspoon minced spring onion
- 1 teaspoon minced ginger
- 1 teaspoon minced garlic
- 1 Szechuan fermented beans ball
- 3 ounces ground pork
- 1 teaspoon chili powder
- 1 tablespoon soy sauce
- ½ teaspoon MSG

Method:

1. Remove bones from codfish. Scrape off scales. Lay the fish on an oval steel plate. Drip wine on top. Steam for 10 minutes over a high flame.
2. Heat oil in a wok. Stir-fry spring onion, ginger, and garlic for a few seconds. Add Szechuan fermented beans ball and ground pork. Stir-fry until the fermented beans ball turns loose and scorched. Add chili powder, soy sauce, and MSG. Stir-fry till the mixture turns crisp.
3. Pour the mixture over the fish. Put the plate on a Wu-Ching burner. Serve.

Notes:

1. Other fish, such as pomfret and sole, can be cooked this way.
2. A Wu-Ching burner is a kind of burner designed to keep the dish warm.

鍋粑蝦仁
Stewed Shelled Shrimps with Kuo-Ba (Crispy Rice)

Ingredients:
8 ounces shelled shrimps
3 ounces peas
6 cups oil
2 cups stock
2 tablespoons cornstarch paste
15 pieces kuo-ba (around 2″ square)

Seasoning (1):
$1/2$ teaspoon salt
2 teaspoons thick cornstarch paste

Seasoning (2):
3 tablespoons tomato sauce
1 teaspoon salt
1 tablespoon sugar
1 tablespoon vinegar
$1/2$ teaspoon MSG

Method:
1. Rinse the shelled shrimps. Marinate in Seasoning (1) for 10 minutes. Rinse the peas. Boil till done. Soak in cold water.
2. Heat oil in a wok. Fry the shrimps until partly cooked. Remove and drain.
3. Save some oil in the wok. Stir-fry shrimps over a high flame quickly till well done. Remove.
4. Bring the stock to a boil. Add Seasoning (2). Return to a boil. Add cornstarch paste. Add shrimps and peas. Mix well. Pour into a soup bowl.
5. Heat oil in the wok. Fry kuo-ba over a high flame till it turns golden brown. Ladle out and drain. (Do not drain too well.) Put in a soup plate. Serve with the bowl of stewed shrimps. To eat, pour the stewed shrimps over the fried kuo-ba.

Notes:
1. You will hear a sizzling sound when pouring the stewed shrimps on the kuo-ba.
2. The golden kuo-ba, the red tomato sauce with green peas, and the sizzling sound make this dish not only delicious, but also pleasant to both the eyes and the ears.

鍋粑作法
How to Make Kuo-Ba
(Crispy Rice)

Kuo-ba is a traditional and unique Chinese food. The Master of Kuo-Ba in Taiwan is Mr. Lin Yang-Yuan. According to Mr. Lin, the typical steps in making kuo-ba are,

1. Choose glutenous rice, which is sticky. Pick out any extraneous matter. Rinse. Soak in water for 2 hours. Pour out some water. Add salt. Steam in a rice cooker.
2. Brush a layer of oil on a wok. Carefully spread the steamed rice evenly on the oiled surface of the wok. Remember to wet the spatula so that the steamed rice won't stick to it.
3. Trim the edge of the layer of steamed rice in the wok. Put it on the stove and bake over a low flame. Turn the wok from time to time so that the steamed rice can be heated evenly. Bake till the side touching the wok turns scorched and is no longer sticky. Remove. Cut into 2″ squares.

4. At this moment, the kuo-ba is still a little bit sticky and wet. Put it on a large round sieve. Lay under the sun to dry.
5. To fry kuo-ba, heat 3 cups oil in a wok to over 400°F. Put kuo-ba in the oil. The moment it contacts the hot oil, it will expand. Turn it over once during frying. Fry till slightly golden brown. Fried kuo-ba can be served with stewed shelled shrimps or stewed seafood, or eaten as is.
6. If you want to preserve kuo-ba for a long time, do not use any oil when baking. Dry it by laying under the sun, then preserve. It can be kept for about one year.

鍋粑三鮮

Stewed Sea Cucumbers, Squid, and Chicken Slices with Kuo-Ba (Crispy Rice)

Ingredients:

2 sea cucumbers (already soaked in water)
2 squids (already soaked in water)
1 ounce ham
1 bamboo shoot
6 mushrooms
6 cups oil
1 ounce chicken slices
4 cups stock
2 teaspoons salt
1 teaspoon MSG
1 tablespoon soy sauce
2 tablespoons cornstarch paste
pea shoots
15 pieces kuo-ba

Method:

1. Rinse sea cucumbers. Cut into 1″-long sections. Rinse squids. Score the insides to make a crisscross pattern. Slice ham into 1″-long sections. Peel bamboo shoot. Cut into 1″ slices. Cut each mushroom in half. Cook these ingredients in boiling water for a short while.

2. Heat 3 tablespoons oil in a wok. Stir-fry sea cucumber, squid, chicken slices, ham slices, bamboo shoot slices, and mushrooms. Mix well. Add stock, salt, MSG, and soy sauce. Bring to a boil over a low flame. Add cornstarch paste. Add pea shoots. Remove when pea shoots are cooked.

3. Heat the remaining in a wok. Fry kuo-ba over a high flame till golden brown. Remove and drain briefly. Put in a soup plate. Serve with the stewed items. To eat, pour the stewed items over the fried kuo-ba.

Note:

The sauce of this dish preserves the original taste of the seafood, which makes it different from the taste of the stewed shelled shrimps, cooked with tomato sauce, sugar, and vinegar.

芙蓉紅蟳

Fu-Yung Red Crabs

Ingredients:

3 red crabs
2 tablespoons wine
4 egg whites
2 teaspoons salt
1 teaspoon MSG
4 tablespoon oil
chicken oil
pea shoots

Method:

1. Rinse the crabs. Brush off dirts from crabs. Remove the gills and the guts. Put in a large bowl. Drip wine on top. Steam for 15 minutes. Remove.
2. Chop off the crabs' legs but save the large claws. Dig meat out of the crabs. Save the back shells. Arrange the shells and the claws on a plate.
3. Beat egg whites until stiff. Mix with crab meat. Add salt and MSG.
4. Heat oil in a wok. Stir-fry the mixture over a high flame till the batter is no longer runny. Remove to a plate, Drip some chicken oil on top. Garnish with scalded pea shoots. Serve.

麻婆豆腐
Ma-Po's Bean Curd

Ingredients:
- 2 bean curds
- 2 tablespoons oil
- 4 ounces ground pork
- 2 cups stock
- 1 tablespoon cornstarch paste

Seasoning (1):
- 2 tablespoons hot bean sauce
- 1 teaspoon minced ginger

Seasoning (2):
- $1/2$ tablespoon soy sauce
- $1/2$ teaspoon MSG
- 1 teaspoon wine

Seasoning (3):
- $1/2$ teaspoon sesame oil
- 1 teaspoon minced spring onion
- 1 teaspoon ground pepper

Method:
1. Cut bean curd into $3/4''$ cubes. Cook in boiling water for a while.
2. Heat oil in a wok. Quickly stir-fry the ground pork with Seasoning (1) till the pork is well cooked. Add stock, bean curd, and Seasoning (2). Simmer over a low flame till there's almost no juice left. Add cornstarch paste. Remove
3. Sprinkle Seasoning (3) on top and serve.

Notes:
1. This dish is considered authentic only if it tastes hot, spicy, and tender at the same time.
2. In the original recipe, ground beef was used instead of ground pork. But most restaurants now use ground pork instead.

豆腐作法

How to Make Bean Curd

Bean curd is very delicious and nutritious. It's made from soybeans, with no artificial flavor or preservatives added.

The Mix-Lien Industries Co. from Shanghai is the most well known bean curd maker in Taiwan. Following are their instructions for making bean curd.

1. Pick over the soybeans. Soak in water till expanded. If the weather is cold, more time will be needed to soak the soybeans; sometimes warm water will be needed.

2. Grind the soaked soybeans to a liquid. Bring the liquid to a boil. Strain out the dregs. (These steps are now taken care of by machines.)

3. Now comes the hardest step, called "dien," meaning "let the bean juice turn solid." To accomplish this step, edilbe plaster has to be added. For 40 pounds of soybeans, you will need 1 pound of plaster. Mix the bean juice with the plaster.

4. Do not stir any more after the "dien" step is done. Let it stand still and it will turn solid in about 5 minutes. Then ladle out the half-solid bean juice carefully and put in a square mold. Spread a piece of cheesecloth on the bottom of the mold first.

5. Fold the cheesecloth toward the center carefully. Remove the frame. Overlap the boards so that the water can be squeezed out.

6. When the water in the bean curd has been squeezed out, put it upside down on another piece of board. Remove the cheesecloth. The delicious tender bean curd is made.

7. The steps for making old bean curd and tender bean curd are very similar. The difference is in the "dien" step. When making tender bean curd, do not stir any more after the bean juice turns half solid. When making old bean curd, you'll have to stir the bean juice again after it turns solid, remove the water that comes out from the second stirring, then put the bean juice in the mold.

紹子烘蛋
Shao-Tsu Omelet

Ingredients:

> 6 eggs
> 4 tablespoons ground pork
> 4 tablespoons minced wood ears
> 4 tablespoons minced Szechuanese
>   preserved mustard head
> $2^{1}/_{2}$ cups oil
> minced spring onion
> 1 cup stock
> 1 teaspoon salt
> $^{1}/_{2}$ teaspoon MSG

Seasoning:

> $^{1}/_{2}$ teaspoon salt
> $^{1}/_{2}$ tablespoon cornstarch

Method:

1. Beat eggs well. Add Seasoning. Mix well. Add 2 tablespoons each of ground pork, minced wood ears, and minced Szechuanese preserved mustard head. Mix well.
2. Heat oil in a wok. Pour the batter into the wok. Fry over a high flame for a while, then switch to a low flame and fry for 3 minutes. The edge of the batter will turn solid and expand. If the center is not expanded, pour a ladle of hot oil on top. Cover the wok. Fry till all the egg batter turns solid and expanded. Turn over carefully. Remove to a round plate when both sides are golden brown. Score in 1 squares.
3. Stir-fry the remaining ground pork with the oil left in the wok. When it becomes loose, add minced wood ears, minced Szechuanese preserved mustard head, and minced spring onion. Stir-fry for a while. Add stock. Bring to a boil. Add salt and MSG. Remove and pour over the omelet. Serve.

八寶豆腐
Ba-Bao Bean Curd

Ingredients:
- 2 bean curds
- 2 cups stock
- 2 teaspoons salt
- 1 teaspoon MSG
- 1 tablespoon cornstarch paste
- chicken oil

Seasoning:
- 1 pork stomach
- 1 sea cucumber (already soaked in water)
- 2 squids (already soaked in water)
- 4 dried black mushrooms
- 1 ounce ham
- 5 canned baby corn ears
- 1 tablespoon shelled broad beans
- 1 tablespoon small dried shrimps

Method:
1. Cut off hard edges and skin of bean curds. Cut into 1″ slices. Rinse pork stomach. Remove all filthy parts from the stomach. Rinse sea cucumber and squids. Soak dried black mushrooms in water till soft. Remove stalks. Cut the above ingredients and the ham into 1″ slices. Slice baby corn into long, thin strips. Cook all ingredients in Seasoning in boiling water for a short time.
2. Bring the stock to a boil. Put bean curd slices in the pot carefully. Arrange the bean curd slices neatly. Bring to a boil over a low flame. Turn off the fire. Remove bean curd carefully to a soup plate.
3. Add Seasoning to the soup left in the pot. Bring to a boil over a high flame. Simmer over low heat for 10 minutes. Add salt and MSG. Add cornstarch paste. Pour over the bean curd. Drip some chicken oil on top. Serve.

Notes:
There are two other ways of making this dish:
1. Cut bean curds into large pieces. Fry with hot oil until light yellow. Remove and drain. Make a large hole in each piece. Stuff with the minced Seasoning. Seal with flour batter. Fry to a golden brown. Pour the juice made from the remaining Seasoning on top of the stuffed bean curd cubes. Serve.
2. Cut off the hard edges and skin of the bean curds. Shred bean curds. Fry until yellow. Remove and drain.

金銀鴿蛋
Gold and Silver Quail Eggs

Ingredients:

    20 quail eggs
    6 cups spiced juice
    1 small taro
    5 cups oil
    cornstarch powder

Method:

1. Boil quail eggs until cooked. Shell the eggs. Put 10 of them in the spiced juice and simmer for 10 minutes.
2. Rinse the taro. Peel. Shred thinly. Put the shreds in a strainer. Heat oil in a wok. Put the strainer with taro shreds in the hot oil to fry till taro shreds turn golden brown. Remove and drain.
3. Add a little bit of water to the cornstarch to make cornstarch paste. Cut each quail egg in half. Glue half a white quail egg to half a brown quail egg with cornstarch paste. Coat the combined egg with cornstarch powder. Arrange the eggs on a plate. Steam for 3 minutes.
4. Put the nest made from fried taro shreds on a plate. Put the eggs in the nest. Garnish with coriander and carved vegetable or fruit. Serve.

Note:

Spiced juice is the soup reserved from some spiced meat dishes, such as Spiced Beef.

豆腐丸子
Bean Curd Balls

Ingredients:

    3 tender bean curds
    3 ounces chicken breast meat
    5 water chestnuts
    1 cup flour
    2 green vegetables
    2 tablespoons cornstarch
    5 cups oil
    5 slices carrot
    1 cup stock
    $1^1/_2$ teaspoons salt
    1 teaspoon MSG
    1 tablespoon cornstarch paste

Method:

1. Cut off hard edges and skin of bean curds. Mash. Mince chicken breast meat. Mince water chestnuts. Mix flour with some water to make a batter. Cut each green vegetable into 4 pieces.
2. Press water from the mushed bean curd. Add minced chicken breast, minced water chestnuts, and cornstarch. Mix well.
3. Heat oil in a wok. Form the mixture into small balls about the size of table tennis balls. Coat each ball with flour batter. Fry until golden brown. Remove and drain.
4. Save some oil in the wok. Stir-fry the green vegetable and carrot till cooked. Add stock, salt, MSG, and the fried bean curd balls. Bring to a boil. Add cornstarch paste. Remove and serve.

熊掌豆腐

Bear Plam Bean Curd

Ingredients:
2 bean curds
4 dried black mushrooms
1 tablespoon dried small shrimps
1 spring onion
4 cups oil
3 slices ginger
5-6 slices ham
1¹⁄₂ cups stock
¹⁄₂ teaspoon MSG
1 tablespoon cornstarch paste

Seasoning:
3 tablespoons soy sauce
1 tablespoon wine
¹⁄₂ teaspoon salt
¹⁄₂ teaspoon sugar

Method:
1. Rinse bean curds. Cut across into 2 pieces, then cut into 12 small pieces. Soak dried black mushrooms in water till soft. Remove stalks. Cut each one into 4 pieces. Rinse the dried small shrimps. Cut spring onion into 1″ sections.
2. Heat oil in a wok. Fry bean curd until golden brown. Remove and drain.
3. Save some oil in the wok. Stir-fry spring onion and ginger for a few seconds. Add bean curd, dried black mushrooms, ham slices, dried shrimp, and stock. (If the stock is not enough to cover all ingredients, you can add more stock.) Add Seasoning. Simmer over a medium flame for 10 minutes.
4. Add MSG when all ingredients are cooked. Add cornstarch paste. Remove and serve.

蘆筍三素

The Three Vegetables Plate

Ingredients:

1 can asparagus
15 green vegetables
10 dried black mushrooms
3 cups stock
1 tablespoon flour
1 tablespoon cornstarch paste
2 teaspoons salt
1 teaspoon MSG
1 teaspoon chicken oil

Method:

1. Drain the asparagus. Cut asparagus into 2″-long sections. Rinse green vegetables. Remove old leaves. Save only the inner parts, about 2″ long. Cut each one lengthwise into 2 long pieces. Cook in boiling water till done. Soak dried black mushrooms in water till soft. Remove stalks.
2. Arrange asparagus, green vegetable, and dried black mushroom on a plate. Carefully invert into a large round strainer.
3. Bring stock to a boil. Put the strainer in and simmer over a low flame for 5-7 minutes. Remove the strainer carefully. Return ingredients to the plate, right side up.
4. Add flour, cornstarch, salt, and MSG to the stock left in the pot. Stir over small flame till sticky. Pour over the vegetables. Drip some chicken oil on top. Serve.

魚香茄餅
Eggplant Patties with Fish-Flavored Sauce

Ingredients:

- 3 ounces ground pork
- 1/2 teaspoon salt
- 1 tablespoon cornstarch
- 1 cup flour
- 2 large eggplants
- 5 cups oil

Seasoning:

- 1 tablespoon minced spring onion
- 1 tablespoon minced ginger
- 1 tablespoon minced garlic
- 1 tablespoon hot bean suace
- 3 tablespoons stock
- 1 tablespoon soy sauce
- 1 teaspoon vinegar
- 1 teaspoon sugar
- 1 teaspoon salt
- 1/2 teaspoon ground pepper
- 1/2 teaspoon MSG
- 1 tablespoon cornstarch paste

Method:

1. Mix ground pork, salt, and cornstarch. Add some water to the flour to make batter.
2. Rinse the eggplants. Cut the stems and the ends. Cut on a slant in 3/4"-thick slices. Score each piece across but do not cut through. Stuff ground pork into each eggplant patty.
3. Heat oil in a wok. Coat the eggplant patty with flour batter. Fry until golden brown. Remove and drain. Arrange on a plate.
4. Mix Seasoning well in a large bowl. Heat 4 tablespoons oil in the wok. Stir-fry Seasoning over a high flame till well mixed. Pour over the fried eggplant patties. Serve.

Note:

Remember to fry the eggplant patties quickly over a high flame, or the patties will turn soft.

青椒茄泥
Eggplant Mash with Green Pepper Sauce

Ingredients:

- 3 eggplants
- 1 small green pepper
- 3 tablespoons oil
- 2 teaspoons minced dried small shrimps
- 1 teaspoon minced Szechuanese preserved mustard head
- 1 teaspoon salt
- 1/2 teaspoon MSG
- minced spring onion
- chicken oil

Method:

1. Rinse the eggplants. Cut off stems, ends, and skin. Cut into 1" slices. Remove stalk from green pepper. Seed. Rinse. Dice.
2. Put eggplant slices in a large bowl. Steam till very soft (about 5 minutes.) Remove. When it gets cold, drain.
3. Heat oil in a wok. Stir-fry minced dried small shrimps, minced Szechuanese preserved mustard head, and eggplant with salt and MSG. Add minced spring onion and green pepper dice. Stir-fry for a while. Remove. Drip some chicken oil on top and serve.

Note:

If small dried shrimps and chicken oil are omitted, this dish is good for vegetarians.

San-Hsia-Kuo

Ingredients:

    1 ounce lean pork
    3 ounces carrot
    3 ounces turnip
    1 Chinese cabbage
    5 cups oil
    2 tablespoon dried chili pieces
    1 tablespoon chili oil
    2 tablespoons stock
    1 teaspoon salt
    1 teaspoon MSG

Method:

1. Slice the pork. Rinse carrot and turnip. Peel. Slice thinly. Use only the stems of the large leaves of the Chinese cabbage. Slice the stems.
2. Heat oil in a wok. Fry the pork slices, the carrot slices, the turnip slices, and the cabbage stem slices for 3 minutes. Remove and drain.
3. Save 3 tablespoons oil in the wok. Stir-fry the dried chili and chili oil for a few seconds. Add stock, salt, MSG and the fried slices. Cover the wok. Simmer for 10 minutes. Remove and serve.

Notes:

1. San-Hsia-Kuo means to fry three different ingredients at the same time. (Carrot slices and turnip slices are considered to be the same ingredient.)
2. To get stems of Chinese cabbage, you can use the leaves removed in preparing the dish Stewed Chinese Cabbage with Three Kinds of Shreds.

Stewed Chinese Cabbage with Three Kinds of Shreds

Ingredients:

    5 dried black mushrooms
    3 ounces ham
    3 ounces chicken breast meat
    4 Chinese cabbages
    3 cups stock
    3 tablespoons oil
    2 teaspoons salt
    1 teaspoon MSG
    2 tablespoons cornstarch paste

Method:

1. Soak dried black mushrooms in water till soft. Remove stalks. Shred the dried black mushrooms, ham, and chicken breast meat. Cook the shreds in boiling water for a while. Remove and drain.
2. Rinse the Chinese cabbages. Remove the larger leaves and save only the 3″-long cabbage hearts. Cut each heart lengthwise into pieces. Arrange in the pot. Add stock. Bring to a boil over a high flame. Lower the flame and simmer for 30 minutes. Take the cabbage out and arrange on a round plate.
3. Heat oil in a wok. Pour the juice of the stewed cabbage into the wok. Add salt, MSG, ham shreds, dired black mushroom shreds, and chicken shreds. Bring to a boil. Add cornstarch paste when all the shreds are well cooked. Pour over the cabbage. Serve.

雞油鮮筍
Bamboo Shoot Slices with Chicken Oil

Ingredients:

>   3 bamboo shoots
>   3 tablespoons oil
> $1/2$ teaspoon salt
>   1 teaspoon MSG
>   2 teaspoons cornstarch paste
>   2 teaspoons chicken oil
>   5 ounces pea shoots

Method:

1. Peel bamboo shoots. Cut into $1/4'' \times 3/8'' \times 2''$ pieces.
2. Cook bamboo shoot slices in boiling water for a while. Remove and drain.
3. Heat oil in a wok. Stir-fry bamboo shoot slices quickly over a high flame. When almost done, add salt, MSG, and cornstarch paste. Mix well, Remove.
4. Drip chicken oil on top. Garnish with boiled pea shoots and serve.

乾煸冬筍

Dry-Fried Bamboo Shoot

Ingredients:
  3 bamboo shoots
  4 cups oil
  1 tablespoon minced dried small shrimps
  1 tablespoon minced ham
  1 teaspoon minced Szechuanese preserved
    mustard head
  1 teaspoon salt
  1/2 teaspoon MSG
  2 teaspoons sugar
  minced spring onion
  stock
  5 ounces pea shoots

Method:
1. Rinse bamboo shoots. Peel. Cut each one into 4 pieces, then cut each piece into 1″-long cubes.
2. Heat oil in a wok. Fry bamboo shoot cubes until brown. Remove and drain.
3. Save some oil in the wok. Stir-fry minced dried small shrimps, minced ham, and minced Szechuanese preserved mustard head for a short while. Add bamboo shoot cubes. Stir-fry with salt, MSG, sugar, and minced spring onion. Mix well. Add stock. Raise the flame and stir-fry till there's no juice left. Remove.
4. Boil pea shoots until cooked. Use to garnish the plate. Serve.

Note:
Remember to cut bamboo shoot to cubes of a uniform size, or the large cubes will be still raw while the smaller cubes are overcooked.

雞火青豆
Stewed Broad Beans with Chicken and Ham

Ingredients:
  4 ounces chicken breast meat
  4 ounces ham
  3 tablespoons lard
  1 spring onion (sectioned)
  2 slices ginger
  5 ounces shelled broad beans
  6 cups oil for frying
  $2\frac{1}{2}$ cups stock
  $\frac{1}{2}$ teaspoon salt
  $\frac{1}{2}$ teaspoon MSG
  $\frac{1}{2}$ tablespoon cornstarch paste

Seasoning:
  $\frac{1}{2}$ egg white
  1 teaspoon cornstarch
  salt
  MSG

Method:
1. Cut chicken breast meat and ham into small cubes the size of the broad beans.
2. Mix chicken dice with Seasoning. Fry in hot oil for a while. Remove and drain.
3. Heat lard in a wok. Stir-fry spring onion and ginger for a few seconds. Remove spring onion and ginger. Add chicken dice, ham dice, broad beans, stock, salt, and MSG. Boil till cooked. Add cornstarch paste. Remove and serve.

成都素燴
Cheng-Du Stewed Vegetables

Ingredients:

> 20 ounces carrot
> 20 ounces turnip
> 2 small potatoes
> 10 dried black mushrooms
> 4 baby leaf mustard plants
> 2 cucumbers
> 3 ounces mushrooms
> 2 ounces lard
> 1 spring onion (sectioned)
> 3 slices ginger
> 3 cups stock
> 4 ounces canned gingko nuts
> $1/2$ teaspoon salt
> $1/2$ teaspoon MSG
> $1/2$ tablespoon cornstarch

Method:

1. Rinse carrot turnip, and potatoes. Peel. Cut into slices $1/4'' \times 2'' \times 2''$. Soak dried black mushrooms in water till soft. Remove stalks. Remove the larger leaves from the leaf mustard. Cut each leaf mustard lengthwide into 2 pieces. Peel cucumbers. Cut into 2"-long strips. Rinse mushrooms.
2. Cook the above ingredients in boiling water for a while. Soak them in cold water. Remove and drain.
3. Heat lard in a wok. Stir-fry spring onion and ginger for a few seconds. Remove spring onion and ginger. Add stock, the boiled ingredients, gingko nuts, salt, and MSG. Simmer over a low flame for 3 minutes.
4. Remove all ingredients. Arrange them in a large bowl. Steam for 15 minutes. Pour it out, upside down, on a large plate.
5. Add cornstarch to the juice left in the wok. Pour over the vegetables. Serve.

砂鍋豆腐
Bean Curd in Earthen Pot

Ingredients:

    8 tender bean curds
    3 ounces pork sinew (already soaked in water)
    2 sea cucumbers (already soaked in water)
    2 squids (already soaked in water)
    1 bamboo shoot
    1 pork stomach
    5 mushrooms
    $1/4$ chicken
    5 cups stock
    1 tablespoon dried small shrimps
    1 tablespoon salt
    1 teaspoon MSG

Method:

1. Cut off hard edges and skin of bean curds. Cut into 1″ cubes. Rinse pork sinew, sea cucumbers, and squids. Cut into 1″ pieces. Rinse bamboo shoot. Peel it. Cut into 1″ pieces. Rinse pork stomach. Cut into 1″ pieces. Cut each mushroom into 2 pieces. Cook these ingredients in boiling water for a while. Remove and drain.
2. Boil chicken in he stock till cooked. Remove chicken. Soak in cold water. Cut into 1″ pieces after it gets cold.
3. Put the above ingredients and dried small shrimps in a large earthen pot. Add stock, salt, and MSG. Bring to a boil over a high flame. Lower the flame and simmer for 1 hour. Serve in the earthen pot. A small burner can be put under the pot to keep it hot during wintertime.

Note:

To clean pork stomach, scrape off the filthy parts from the outer layer. Cut it open and scrape off the filthy parts from the inner layer. Boil for a while. Rub the stomach with salt, vinegar, spring onion, and ginger to remove its offensive smell.

原盅豆芽排骨湯
Bean Sprouts and Pork Ribs Soup

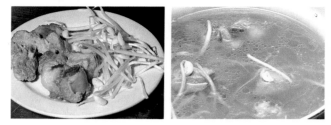

Ingredients:

    $2^1/_2$ pounds pork ribs
    10 ounces bean sprouts
    6 cups stock
    5 slices ginger
    1 tablespoon salt
    1 teaspoon MSG

Method:

1. Chop pork ribs into 2″ cubes. Cook in boiling water for a while. Remove and drain. Rinse bean sprouts and trim.
2. Pour stock into a pot. Add the ribs and ginger. Bring to a boil over a high flame. Lower the flame and simmer for 40-50 minutes. Add bean sprouts, salt, and MSG. Simmer for 20 minutes. Pour into a soup bowl. Serve.

酸辣湯
Hot and Sour Soup

Ingredients:

    3 ounces pork blood curd
    3 ounces bean curd
    2 wood ears
    $1/4$ sea cucumber
    3 cups stock
    1 ounce pork shreds
    1 egg, well beaten
    $1/2$ tablespoon cornstarch paste
    sesame oil

Seasoning (1):

    $1/2$ teaspoon salt
    $1/2$ teaspoon MSG
    $1/2$ tablespoon soy sauce
    2 ounces ground pepper

Seasoning (2):

    2 teaspoons minced spring onion
    2 teaspoons minced ginger
    1 tablespoon vinegar

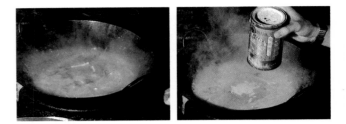

Method:

1. Shred the pork blood curd, bean curd, wood ears, and sea cucumber. Add to stock along with shredded pork and bring to a boil.
2. Add Seasoning (1). Mix well, then add egg. Stir the soup when adding the egg. Add cornstarch paste. Put Seasoning (2) in a large soup bowl. Pour the soup into the bowl. Drip sesame oil on top. Serve.

Note:

The quantity of pepper and vinegar can be adjusted to your taste.

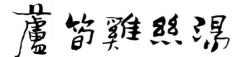

Asparagus and Chicken Shreds Soup

Ingredients:

4 ounces chicken breast meat
1 can asparagus
1 ounce button mushrooms
1 ounce pea shoots
6 cups stock
1 teaspoon salt
$1/2$ teaspoon MSG
1 teaspoon chicken oil

Seasoning:

2 egg whites
$1/2$ teaspoon salt
2 tablespoons cornstarch

Method:

1. Slice chicken breast meat into thin pieces, then cut to 1"-long shreds. Marinate in Seasoning (1) for 20 minutes. Drain the asparagus. Cut into 1" sections. Rinse button mushrooms. Drain. Pick off the old parts of the pea shoots.

2. Cook chicken shreds in boiling water till done. (When it becomes loose, remove.) Drain.
3. Put stock in a pot. Add chicken shreds, asparagus, and button mushrooms. Bring to a boil. Add salt, MSG, and pea shoots. Return to a boil. Remove.
4. Drip chicken oil on top and serve.

四寶元盅
Four-Treasures Soup

Ingredients:

> 1 ounce ham
> 1 ounce chicken breast meat
> 1 pork stomach
> 1 turnip
> 1 dried black mushroom
> 2 eggs
> 4 tablespoons ground pork
> pea shoots
> sesame oil
> 6 cups stock

Method:

1. Slice ham and chicken into 1″ pieces. Rinse the pork stomach. Slice into 1″ pieces. Rinse the turnip. Peel. Cut into 1″-long strips. Soak the dried black mushroom in water till soft. Remove the stalk.
2. Beat eggs well. Make a thin egg pancake from the eggs. Put ground pork on two side of the egg pancake. Roll from the two sides toward the center. Steam for 10 minutes. Slice on a slant after it cools off.
3. Have a medium-size soup bowl ready. Put the dried black mushroom in the center of the bottom of the bowl. Arrange ham slices, chicken slices, pork stomach slices, and the stuffed egg pancake slices neatly in the bowl. Stuff the center with turnip strips.
4. Steam for 7-8 minutes. Pour out, upside down, into a large soup bowl. Garnish with boiled pea shoots. Drip sesame oil on top. Pour in the boiling stock. Serve.

Notes:

1. See the note on p. 99 for how to clean a pork stomach.
2. To make the egg pancake, brush some oil on a pan. Heat over a low flame. Pour the egg batter in carefully, tilting the pan so the batter covers it evenly. When the edge of the pancake curls up, remove carefully.

酸菜肚片湯
Sour Cabbage and Pork Stomach Slices Soup

Ingredients:

1 pork stomach
5 ounces sour cabbage
1 bamboo shoot
6 cups stock
1 teaspoon salt
1/2 teaspoon MSG
sesame oil

Method:

1. Rinse the pork stomach. Cook briefly in boiling water. Slice into 1″ pieces. Rinse the sour cabbage. Drain. Cut its stem parts into 1″ slces. Peel the bamboo shoot. Cut into 1″ slices.
2. Bring the stock to a boil. Add pork stomach slices, sour cabbage slices, and bamboo shoot slices. Return to a boil. Add salt and MSG. Lower the flame and simmer for 10-15 minutes. When the pork stomach slices are wellcooked, turn off the heat. Pour into a soup bowl.
3. Drip some sesame oil on top. Serve.

Notes:

1. See the note on p. 99 for how to clean a pork stomach.
2. Sour cabbage is salty, so taste the soup before adding salt.

紅燒川味牛肉麵
Beef Noodles, Szechuaness Style

Ingredients:
- 4-5 pounds beef
- 10 ounces old ginger
- 1 ounce garlic
- 3 tablespoons wine
- 1 cup hot bean sauce
- $\frac{1}{2}$ cup chili oil
- 1 tablespoon salt
- 6 cups stock
- 3 ounces noodles

Seasoning (1):
- 2 tablespoons sugar
- 3 tablespoons oil

Seasoning (2):
- 1 teaspoon salt
- $\frac{1}{2}$ teaspoon MSG
- 1 tablespoon soy sauce
- minced spring onion

Method:
1. Cut off fatty parts from the beef. Cut into 1″ × 3″ pieces. Cook in boiling water. When the color of the beef turns light, remove and drain. Rinse the ginger. Slice. Peel the garlic. Flatten with a cleaver.
2. Simmer Seasoning (1) over a low flame till thick. Add the beef and wine. Switch to a medium flame. Stir-fry well. Add hot bean sauce and chili oil. Stir-fry well.
3. Pour into a pot. Add salt, ginger, garlic, and stock. Simmer over a low flame for 3-5 hours.
4. Put Seasoning (2) in a soup bowl.
5. Bring water to a boil. Shake the noodles to separate, then put in the boiling water. Return to a boil. Lower the flame and simmer till the noodles are cooked. Pour $\frac{1}{2}$ cup noodle soup into the bowl with Seasoning (2). Remove noodles to the bowl. Add some stewed beef and juice. Serve.

Notes:
1. Quantities of the ingredients used can be adjusted to taste.
2. Frozen beef can be used.
3. Stir the cooked noodles to loosen when putting in the bowl, or they will get sticky after a while.

擔擔麵
Dan-Dan Noodles

Ingredients:
- 1 ounce noodles

Seasoning:
- 2 teaspoons minced preserved mustard head
- 1 tablespoon sesame sauce
- 1 tablespoon lard
- 1 teaspoon salt
- 1 teaspoon MSG
- minced spring onion
- 1 tablespoon soy sauce
- 1 tablespoon peanut powder
- stock

Method:
1. Mix Seasoning well in a bowl.
2. Cook noodles in boiling water. Add to the bowl with mixed Seasoning. Mix well. Serve.

Note:
This makes one serving. For many people, you can mix Seasoning according to above instructions in separate bowl, boil the noodles at one time, then remove the cooked noodles to each bowl.

泡菜
Pickled Vegetables

Ingredients:
- 1 cabbage
- 2 turnips
- 5 chilies
- 1 ounce ginger
- 2 tablespoons vinegar
- 2 tablespoons salt
- 1 tablespoon sugar
- 2 cups cold boiled water

Method:
1. Rinse the cabbage leaves. Wipe dry. Tear into pieces. Rinse the turnip. Peel. Slice into 1″ pieces. Rinse the chilies. Remove stalks and seeds. Slice. Rinse the ginger. Peel, then slice.
2. Put all ingredients in a clean, nongreasy earthen jar. Cover the jar. Let stand for 2 days, then serve.

Notes:
1. A glass jar can be used instead of the earthen jar, but the jar used has to be very clean. If the jar is greasy, the pickled vegetables will turn rotten.
2. After the pickled vegetables are eaten up, the juice can be reused. Just add cabbage to the juice. If the weather is hot, put it in the refrigerator.
3. The quantity of seasonings used can be adjusted to your taste.

蕃茄牛肉麵
Stewed Tomatoes and Beef Noodles

Ingredients:

        4-5 pounds beef
        5-6 tomatoes
        3 spring onions
        3 spring onions
        5 ounces old ginger
        1 ounce garlic
        2 tablespoons peanut oil
        3 tablespoons sugar color
        1 cup wine
        2 teaspoons salt
        2 teaspoons MSG
        1 cup soy sauce
        5 cups stock
        3 ounces noodles

Method:

1. Rinse the beef. Cut into 1″ cubes. Cook in boiling water for a while. When the color of the beef turns light, remove and drain. Rinse the tomatoes. Remove the stems. Cut into small cubes. Rinse the spring onions. Cut into pieces 1″ long. Rinse the ginger. Cut into 1″ pieces. Peel the garlic, then pat it flat.
2. Heat peanut oil in a wok. Stir-fry the tomatoes and sugar color for a while. Add the beef and wine. Stir-fry till sugar color tints the beef. Add spring onions, ginger, garlic, salt, and MSG. Stir-fry well.
3. Pour the above ingredients into a pot. Add soy sauce and stock. Simmer over a low flame for 6-8 hours.
4. Bring a pot of water to a boil. Boil the noodles and remove to a bowl. Add beef and the soup. Serve.

Notes:

1. Fresh beef will need 2 to 3 more hours to cook than frozen beef.
2. If you like hot flavor, you can add chili oil before eating.
3. See note 1 on p. 47 for how to prepare sugar color.

老張担担麵
Lao-Chang's Dan-Dan Mien

Ingredients:
1 ounce noodles

Seasoning:
2 teaspoons minced preserved mustard head
1 tablespoon sesame sauce
minced spring onion
1 teaspoon minced garlic
1 teaspoon salt
$\frac{1}{2}$ teaspoon MSG
$\frac{1}{2}$ teaspoon sugar
$\frac{1}{2}$ teaspoons vinegar
1 teaspoon ground pepper
1 teaspoon lard
1 tablespoon stock

Method:
1. Mix Seasoning well. Put the mixture in a bowl.
2. Cook noodles in boiling water. Remove to the bowl with the Seasoning. Mix well. Serve.

Note:
Lao-Chang is a very famous cook who is an expert in making beef noodles and Dan-Dan Mien in Taiwan.

炸元宵
Fried Yuan-Hsiao

Ingredients:
- 1 package glutenous rice powder
- 4 ounced sweetened mashed black dates
- white sesame seeds
- oil for frying

Method:
1. Add hot water to the glutenous rice powder. Knead till no longer sticky. Divide mashed black dates into 20 parts. Roll each part into a small ball.
2. Rub the glutenous rice powder dough to a stick of 1″ diameter. Divide into 20 parts.
3. Wrap each mashed black dates ball with a piece of glutenous rice powder dough. Coat with white sesame seeds.
4. Heat oil for frying. Fry yuan-hsiao over small flame. Keep stirring during frying. Remove when the color turns light brown. Drain. Arrange on a plate. Serve.

Notes:
1. Yuan-hsiao is the Chinese name for stuffed glutenous rice powder balls.
2. Mashed red beans and mashed sesame seeds can be used to replace mashed black dates.

拔絲香蕉
Maltose-Coated Bananas

Ingredients:
- 3 large bananas
- 2 eggs
- 1 cup flour
- 6 cups oil
- 2 teaspoons black sesame seeds

Seasoning:
- 6 tablespoons granulated sugar
- 2 cups water
- 1 tablespoon maltose

Method:
1. Peel the bananas. Cut into large cubes. Beat the eggs well and mix with flour.
2. Simmer Seasoning in a pot over a low flame till it turns light brown.
3. When the sugar syrup is almost ready, heat oil in a wok. Coat banana cubes with the batter. Fry to golden brown. Remove. Put fried banana cubes in the sugar syrup. Mix well.
4. Sprinkle black sesame seeds on top. Serve.

Notes:
1. This dessert tastes best when it cools down a little bit.
2. Do not let it get completely cold, or it will be hard to eat because the syrup turns solid.

甜燒白

Tien-Shao-Bai

Ingredients:

2¹/₂ pounds pork belly
2 teaspoons sugar color
8 cups oil
8 ounces mashed red beans
4 ounces glutenous rice
4 ounces lard
10 ounces granulated sugar
4 ounces peanut powder

Method:

1. Remove hair from the skin of the pork belly. Rinse. Boil until cooked. Remove and drain. Brush sugar color on the skin.
2. Heat oil in a wok. Fry the pork until golden brown. Remove and drain. Cut into 1¹/₄"-wide pieces. Score crosswide but do not cut through the skin. Stuff 3 teaspoons of mashed read beans into each pork slice.
3. Steam the glutenous rice until cooked. Mix the steamed rice with lard and 5 ounces granulated sugar.
4. Arrange the pork slices in a bowl. Put the steamed rice on top. Steam for 30 minutes.
5. Invert onto a plate. Mix peanut powder and the remaining granulated sugar. Sprinkle the mixture on top. Serve.

Note:

See note 1 on p. 47 for how to prepare sugar color.

桔薈湯元

Soup of Mixed Fruits and Tang-Yuan

Ingredients:
$^1/_2$ package glutenous rice powder
1 can mixed fruits
6 cups hot water
sugar

Method:
1. Add hot water to the glutenous rice powder. Knead till no longer stickly. Rub to a stick of $^3/_8$" diameter. Divide into many small pieces, each about the size of a thumb. Rub each into a small ball.
2. Drain the juice from the can of mixed fruits. Put the mixed fruits in a large soup bowl. Add hot water and sugar. Mix well.
3. Bring water to a boil. Put the small balls (tang-yuan) in the boiling water. Boil till the tang-yuan float. Remove and drain. Put in the bowl with mixed fruits. Serve.

Note:
This dessert can be served hot or cold. If you want to serve it cold, just put the mixed fruits with hot water and sugar in the refrigerator; add tang-yuan before serving.

紅油抄手
Wontons in Chili Oil

Ingredients:
    1 ounce meat stuffing
    10 wonton skins

Seasoning:
    2 teaspoons sweet soy sauce
    1 tablespoon chili oil
    1 tablespoon minced garlic
    1 teaspoon minced spring onion
    1 teaspoon vinegar
    1 teaspoon MSG
    ground pepper

Method:
1. See Ma-La Dumplings for how to prepare meat stuffing.
2. Wrap 1 teaspoon of meat stuffing with a piece of wonton skins. Fold it in the shape of a triagle, then fold the bottom up toward the end; finally fold the left side toward the right side.
3. Mix Easoning well. Put the mixture in a soup bowl.
4. Bring water to a boil. Put in wontons. Bring to a boil. Remove wontsons to the bowl with Seasoning. Serve.

Notes:
1. Szechuanese call wontons Chao-Shou but Fukienese call them Bien-Shih.
2. Sweet soy sauce is a special product of Szechuan Province. It is made by simmering ordinary soy sauce with brown sugar, clove, dried orange peels, and other Chinese flavorings.

麻辣餃
Ma-La Dumplings

Ingredients:
    1 cup flour
    1 egg
    3 ounces pork

Seasoning (1):
    $^{1}/_{2}$ egg
    $^{1}/_{2}$ teaspoon ground pepper
    1 teaspoon salt
    MSG
    sesame oil

Seasoning (2):
    2 teaspoons soy sauce
    1 tablespoon chili oil
    1 teaspoon minced dried preserved cabbage
    1 teaspoon ground pepper
    vinegar
    MSG

Method:
1. Mix flour with beaten egg well. Add water to make dough. Let stand for 10 minutes. Knead to a stick of $^{3}/_{4}''$ diameter. Cut into $^{3}/_{8}''$-long sections. Roll each section with a rolling pin into a thin, round piece of 2" diameter.
2. Chop the pork finely. Mix with Seasoning (1) to make meat stuffing.
3. Wrap $1^{1}/_{2}$ teaspoons meat stuffing with a piece of dumpling skin.
4. Mix Seasoning (2) well to make ma-la juice (the hot and spicy sauce). Put the mixture in a bowl.
5. Bring water to a boil. Put dumplings in the pot. Bring to a boil again. Remove. Put into the bowl with Seasoning (2). Serve.

Notes:
1. The size of the dumplings in this dish is quite small. If it's not for banquet, you can make larger ones.
2. If you make larger dumplings, remember to add cold water after first boiling. Remove the dumplings after the second boiling.
3. The quantity for the meat stuffing above is for 10-12 small dumplings. If you want to make more, just increase the ingredients proportionally.

酸辣麵
Hot and Sour Noodles

Ingredients:
> 1 cup flour
> 1 egg

Seasoning:
> 2 teaspoons soy sauce
> 1 tablespoon chili oil
> 1 tablespoon dark vinegar
> 2 teaspoons minced dried preserved cabbage
> minced spring onion
> 2 teaspoons MSG
> 1 teaspoon ground pepper

Method:
1. Mix flour with beaten egg. Add enough water to make dough. Knead till the dough gets elastic. Roll into a large, round piece 1/8″ thick. Fold it. Shred thinly to make noodles.
2. Mix Seasoning well to make hot and sour juice. Put in a bowl.
3. Bring water to a boil. Put noodles in. Return to a boil over a high flame. Lower the flame. Simmer till cooked. Remove and drain. Put the bowl with the hot and sour juice. Serve.

Seasonings Used in a Szechuanese Restaurant

①②③④ ⑤⑥⑦⑧⑨ ⑩⑪⑫⑬⑭ ⑮⑯⑰⑱ ⑲⑳㉑㉒

1. tomato sauce
2. peppercorns
3. rice wine
4. salt
5. dried chilies
6. minced spring onion
7. sugar color
8. sesame oil
9. sweet flour sauce (sweet bean sauce)
10. stock
11. minced ginger
12. white granulated sugar
13. soy sauce
14. chili sauce
15. minced garlic
16. fermented rice
17. MSG
18. chicken oil
19. pepper powder
20. sections of spring onion and ginger
21. vinegar
22. salt

Seasonings Used in the Family Kitchen for Szechuanese Dishes

①②③④ ⑤⑥⑦⑧

1. hot bean sauce
2. bean sauce
3. sesame sauce (sesame paste)
4. chili oil
5. hot turnips
6. chili sauce
7. chili sauce with black beans
8. sweet flour sauce (sweet bean sauce)

Index I   The Chef and His Dishes

1. Jzyy Yuan Restaurant

Jzyy Yuan's Chung-Shan Branch is located at Chung-Shan N. Road, one of the major roads in Taipei. Besides the Chung-Shan Branch, other restaurants in the Jzyy Yuan Chain Stores are the Jzyy Yuan's Nanking Branch and Ta Shun Restaurant.

Its busy commercial environment together with its chef, Mr. Tseng Chien, are the reasons for its success. Mr. Tseng is a native of Cheng-Du County, Szechuan Province. He spent his early days in the army and is now working full-time in Jzyy Yuan's kitchen. Jzyy Yuan is famous for its homemade dishes, which are authentic and never greasy.

With many international hotels around, Jzyy Yuan has many foreign guests. To host its international guests, Jzyy Yuan is decorated in a pure Chinese way. But its VIP room is decorated in European style. Besides a family dining area, banquet rooms are also available. Delicious dishes, elegant environment, and polite service can guarantee your satisfaction if you dine at Jzyy Yuan.

2. Fortune Restaurant

Its has been a long time since Fortune Restaurant started its business at its present location at Chung-Hsiao E. Road. Ground floor is the dining area for 150 people. If you do not want to be disturbed, there are 23 private rooms of different sizes from which to choose on the first floor.

Fortune's manager, Mr. Wang Kuang-Fu, a generous and responsible person, has been in the business for 30 years.

His guidance and the dishes of the chef, Mr. Chen Tzu-Yi, a native of Szechuan Province, have charmed many gourmets who dined at Fortune. Fortune's Strange-Flavored Chicken, Minced Garlic with White Pork, and the hard-to-prepare Bar-B-Qued Crispy Pork Ribs are the three major dishes that attract regular guests and many foreigners to dine at Fortune time after time.

3. Rong Shing Restaurant

Although Mr. Wu Shao-Chen, the chef of Rong Shing, is very hard on the training of apprentices, all his students call him "sir" and respect him very much. Besides make improvements on the cooking method, he also pays a lot of attentions to the art of fruit and vegetable carving and food decorating. He said, "Preparing dishes is same as painting; tasting food is just like enjoying a piece of artwork. This is why cooking is also an art form."

His fame is spread to other parts of the world by his students, who are now the chefs in many famous restaurants all over the world.

On the ground floor of Rong Shin, there are 36 tables of various capacity. And there are a total of 20 private and elegant rooms designed for banquet use in the basement. Located in the busy commercial area, its business is always good, though its dishes are in a slightly higher price range. A lot of tourists, especially those from Japan and Europe, like to dine here during their stay in Taipei.

4. Lien An Restaurant

Lien-An is the largest of the four Szechuanese restaurants we introduce in this book. It is a five-story building with area about 18,000 square feet. Ground floor is the family dining area, with 24 tables of various sizes. During lunchtime, the ground floor is always busy. There are 16 nicely decorated rooms on both the first floor and second floor for private gathering or banquet. Its third floor is a large banquet room suitable for weddings or birthday parties. It can be partitioned into small rooms if necessary. The fourth floor is the kitchen where all the delicous dishes are prepared.

Lien An's chef, Mr. Wai Cheng-Hsuan, a native of Chungking, Szechuan Province, earned his fame when he was still in Szechuan. He is now one of the leading chefs in Taiwan for Szechuanese dishes. All his students respect him very much. His students are now all over the world, working as chefs in many major restaurants. He is very admirable and devoted. If you go to his kitchen, you'll notice that everything is in good order and every one in the kitchen is doing his or her job according to Mr. Wai's instructions. He is now 72 years old but still strong and healthy. Working full time at Lien An, Mr. Wai said he still has a long way to go.

5. Hsiao-Wai Szechuanese Restaurant

The chef of Hsiao-Wai, Mr. Wai Teh-Rong, is also the owner of the restaurant. He is a native of Taiwan. But the reason that he and his wife can manage a Szechuanese restaurant so successfully is that Mr. Wai was the apprentice of several famous Szechuanese chefs when he was young, and, therefore, learned the typical ways of cooking Szechuanese food. He started his own business seven years ago and is now very successfully.

Located at the corner of Roosevelt Road and King-Hua Street, Hsiao-Wai is the best Szechuanese restaurant around that area to serve its guests, it has 11 workers in the kitchen and 6 waitresses. During lunch and dinner hours, all workers are busy serving and cooking and there are always some guests standing and waiting to be seated. Its Stewed Pork Intestine over Wu-Ching Burner, Steamed Pork Ribs Wrapped in Lotus Leaves, Carp in Hot Bean Sauce, Stewed Bean Curd, and Soup of Peas and Pork Stomach Slices are all worth tasting.

6. The Old Mr. Cheng of Yung-Kang Street

It is only a modest foodstand at the corner of Yuan-Kang Park. Mr. Cheng starts his daily business at 6 in the afternoon and sells only Beef Noodles, Beef Tendon Noodles, Dan-Dan Noodles, and Pickled Vegetables. Mr. Cheng's first name is Yun-lin. He's a native of Chungking, Szechuan Province. Although his noodles are quite expensive, the stand is always busy. Selling noodles for more than 20 years at the same spot is a fact that explains how good his noodles are.

Mr. Cheng used to work alone. But in order to cope up with the busier and busier business, he now has two assistants. We asked Mr. Cheng his secret of cooking noodles so delicious. His answer is "Nothing worth mentioning really. I just use more old ginger and garlic and can control the flame properly."

7. Lao-Chang's Dan-Dan Mien

The chef and owner of Lao-Chang, Mr. Ke Keng-Sheng, is a native of Kiangsu Province. You might wonder howcome the family of the owner is Ke while the name of the store is Lao-Chang. It is because the original owner of this store was a Mr. Chang, who began his business at Tung-Men market, then moved to the corner of Jen-Ai Road and Han-Chou S. Road. Lao-Chang's noodles were so famous that even prestigious people came to the small and crowded store to dine. In order to accommodate more guests, Lao-Chang moved again to its present address at Lane 101 of Han-Chou S. Road. It now has 12 tables and 5 waiters. Mr. Chang retired around two years ago and left the store to Mr. Ke.

After Mr. Ke took over the business, he still kept the store name and the same taste. Besides the most welcomed Stewed Tomatoes and Beef Noodles, there are more than 10 other kinds of noodles and the delcious Steamed Pork Ribs and Steamed Pork Intestine served at Lao-Chang's.

8. Szechuan Wu Chao-Shou

Across Fortune Restaurant is the Szechuan Wu Chao-Shou, a small but famous restaurant serving Szechuanese food. Its branch store is by the New Park with 13 tables.

Wu Chao-Shou is famous for its small dishes, such as Dried-Broiled Yellow Fish, To-To Chicken, Dried-Fried Beef, and the dishes made of Kung-Pao Sauce, and flour products, such as Ma-La Dumplings and Wontons in Chili oil.

Wu Chao-Shou's chef, Mr. Chang Chih-Kuo, is a native of Szechuan Province, who started his career at Wu Chao-Shou after he retired from the army. Long training and his creativity make Wu Chao-Shou the most successful restaurant compared with other restaurants of the same size. Some people said the Hot and Sour Noodles at Wu Chao-Shou can even cure your cold, no matter how serious it is.

Index II Other Recipes of Szechuanese Dishes in Highlight's Culinary Series